THEIR ROYAL HIGHNESSES

THE DUKE

and

DUCHESS OF YORK

THEIR ROYAL HIGHNESSES

THE DUKE
and
DUCHESS OF YORK

CHRISTOPHER WARWICK AND VALERIE GARNER

SIDGWICK & JACKSON
LONDON

First published in Great Britain in 1986
by Sidgwick and Jackson Limited

Designed by Laurence Bradbury/Roy Williams

Picture Research by Deborah Pownall

ISBN 0–283–99386–3

Colour separations by Anglia Reproductions,
Witham, Essex
Printed in England by Jolly & Barber Limited,
Rugby, Warwickshire
and bound by R.J. Acford,
Chichester, Sussex
for Sidgwick and Jackson Limited
1 Tavistock Chambers, Bloomsbury Way
London WC1A 2SG

PICTURE ACKNOWLEDGEMENTS

Sidgwick and Jackson has made every effort to trace the photographers of illustrations in the book. We apologize if there are any copyright holders who have not been acknowledged. The Publishers would like to thank the following who have been particularly helpful in supplying pictures:

Colour pictures
BTA (Eric Rowell): 39, 50; Camera Press: 10 (Terence Donovan), 78 (bottom), 91 (Terence Donovan), 131 (Norman Parkinson), 145 (Gene Nocon), 146 (Terence Donovan), 147 (Terence Donovan), ff162; Lionel Cherruault: 156; Fox Photos Ltd: 55, 67, 75, 126 (right); Tim Graham: 18, 23, 30 (bottom), 31, 42, 70, 74 (top and bottom), 111, 143 (top), 149, 151 (bottom), 157, 160 (right), 161, ff162; Anwar Hussein: 62, 79 (left), 86 (top and bottom), 87, 102, 106, 142, ff162; Illustrated London News: 15, 51, 119, 123; LNS: 134, 143 (bottom); Palavtetaan Suomen Kuvapalveluun: 139; Photographers International: 22 (bottom), 26 (bottom), 38, 94, 159, 160 (left), ff162; Rex Features: 19, 26 (top), 34 (bottom), 35, 63, 78 (top), 79 (right), 82 (top left), 83, 90, 98, 103, 107, 110, 111, 154, ff162; John Scott: 22 (top), 54 (top and bottom), 58 (bottom), 66; *Sunday Times*: ff162; Syndication International: 14, 27, 34 (top), 130, 138 (bottom), 150 (top), 151 (top), ff162; Albert Watson: ff162; Roy Williams: 82 (top right).

Black and white pictures
Alpha: 30 (left) (Alan Davidson), 89, 104; BBC Hulton Picture Library: 116, 117; BTA: 40 (Barry Hicks); Camera Press: 37, 45, 48 (top), 53, 59, 65, 68, 77, 80, 92 (left), 101, 126 (left), 144 (top and bottom); Central Press Photos Ltd: 49, 122; Lionel Cherruault: 136; Fox Photos Ltd: 44 (top), 73, 132; Tim Graham: 85, 97, 105, 108 (top right), 109 (bottom right), 138 (top), 158 (bottom); Anwar Hussein: 61 (top), 100, 108 (bottom); Illustrated London News: 121, 124, 125, 126, 128, 129 (left), 153 (Ed Pritchard); Keystone Press Agency Ltd: 52 (top and bottom), 69, 88 (left); KOPZ: 60; LNS: 141 (Ian Swift); Mansell Collection: 118; Desmond O'Neill: 17 (top and bottom), 20, 21, 25 (top and bottom), 28, 29, 61 (bottom); Photo Source: 44 (bottom), 46, 56, 81; Photographers International: 109 (top and bottom left), 158 (top); Popperfoto: 47, 48 (bottom), 57, 58 (top), 81, 84, 92 (right); Press Association: 64; Rex Features: 24, 32 (bottom), 72, 76, 82, 88 (right), 93, 108 (top right), 137, 152, 155 (Carraro); John Scott: 32 (top), 112, 113; Syndication International: 12, 13, 14 (top), 16 (top and bottom), 36, 41, 129 (right), 140.

Illustrations for Chapter 7 were chosen after this page went to press but are acknowledged as occurring on pages ff162.

For CLS, KMU, RIW
and LAB

CONTENTS

INTRODUCTION

Three weeks before he led his bride down the Nave of Westminster Abbey to the strains of the 'Triumphal March' from Elgar's opera *Caractacus* and the current royal favourite 'Crown Imperial' by Sir William Walton – chosen by the Prince of Wales for his own wedding in 1981 – Prince Andrew, the new Duke of York, publicly confessed to being assailed by fits of pre-wedding nerves.

'I would love to get 23 July out of the way,' he told a BBC news team when he joined other members of his family at a celebrity clay pigeon shoot near Chester. Today the 'ordeal', as Princess Alexandra referred to her wedding at Westminster Abbey in April 1963, is safely behind the Queen's second son and the former Miss Sarah Ferguson – even if the greater ordeal of married life in one of the world's most public arenas is about to unfold before them.

Five years ago, the wedding of the Prince and Princess of Wales was arguably the greatest royal occasion Britain had witnessed since the Coronation of the present Queen twenty-eight years before. Declared a public holiday, Wednesday 29 July 1981 found spectators in their tens of thousands jamming the long processional route from Buckingham Palace to St Paul's Cathedral, while around the world in some 104 countries, 750 million people sat in front of their television screens, transfixed by the scenes of pomp and pageantry, relayed 'live' from London.

At the heart of the wedding celebrations lay, of course, a solemn, if extremely public, affirmation before God of intensely private emotions. As such, despite the high theatricality of the event and the awe-inspiring setting of Wren's monumental cathedral, the royal marriage service varied little from that known to untold millions who choose to plight their troth either to other in the most traditional of all rituals.

If Prince Charles's wedding amounted to pure fantasy, however – and anything less than a Hollywood-style production for the Heir to the Throne might have seemed inappropriate – the wedding of Andrew and Sarah was, by virtue of its relative unimportance, a rather more modest affair. In the days after the engagement was announced the public became totally absorbed with the romance of Andrew and 'Fergie'. As a result, people forgot that public holidays are only ever declared for the most significant of occasions. So many were heard to bemoan the fact that they were not given the day off work to join in the celebrations surrounding *the* royal event of 1986. Some even felt rather cheated by the absence of pre-wedding festivities, such as the great firework display staged in Hyde Park, London, the night before Prince Charles's wedding, and the dramatic lighting of a series of celebratory bonfires throughout the British Isles. Yet, for all that, the air of happy anticipation and tense excitement felt among the crowds

The Duke and Duchess of York, 23 July 1986

on 23 July was just as momentous as it always is on occasions that call into play the unrivalled magnificence of British royal ceremonial.

In this book Valerie Garner and I have attempted to evoke something of the atmosphere of the royal wedding day itself to serve as a colourful and permanent reminder of a particularly memorable occasion. Yet, while the emphasis, quite naturally, has been placed very largely on Wednesday 23 July, supported and enhanced by some of the most glorious colour photographs of the great day, we have also endeavoured to complete the scene by recreating – in words and pictures – the lives of the royal couple from their very earliest days right up to the present.

Christopher Warwick
24 July 1986

SARAH

BRITAIN'S NEW PRINCESS, THE FORMER SARAH FERGUSON, HAD SOME EVENTFUL UPS AND DOWNS IN HER TWENTY-SIX YEARS BEFORE SHE MARRIED PRINCE ANDREW. THERE WAS THE INITIAL UNHAPPINESS AND INSECURITY FOLLOWING THE BREAK-UP OF HER PARENTS' MARRIAGE WHEN SHE WAS THIRTEEN. THEN, IN HER INDEPENDENT TWENTIES, SHE HAD SOME HEARTBREAK OF HER OWN WITH THE END OF A SERIOUS LOVE AFFAIR.

THESE AND OTHER FACETS OF HER LIFE MAY BE REFLECTED IN THE MOTTO SHE CHOSE FOR HER PERSONAL COAT OF ARMS: 'OUT OF ADVERSITY HAPPINESS GROWS.'

When Charles II, from whom the newest member of the royal family is descended through no less than three of his most beautiful mistresses – Lucy Walters, Louise de Kéroualle, Duchess of Portsmouth, and Barbara Villiers, Duchess of Cleveland – was born in May 1630, 'a bright constellation shone in the mid-day sky'.

No such heavenly welcome as the planet Venus greeted his descendant Sarah Margaret Ferguson, the future wife of Prince Andrew, when she was born in a

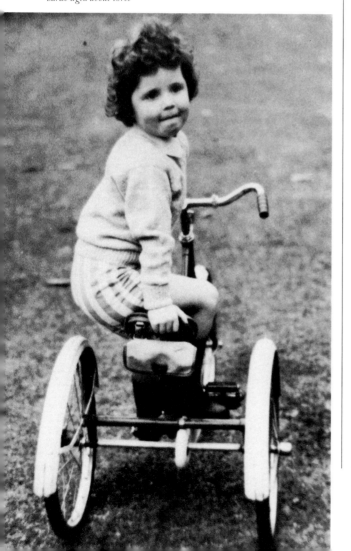

Sarah aged about three

simply furnished nursing-home at 27 Welbeck Street in the heart of central London. Nor did she make headline news like her future husband, Prince Andrew, who had the distinction of being the first baby to be born to a reigning sovereign for over a hundred years.

Yet if Sarah's birth was a relatively obscure affair, the infant with hair as vividly red as the leaves then carpeting the royal parks announced her arrival most vigorously at three minutes past nine on the morning of 15 October 1959.

To her delighted young parents, Susan and Ronald Ferguson, that first strong cry held no hint of their child's future royal role. But it was very much in character. 'Fergie', as she was to be known throughout her childhood, and later, after her engagement to Prince Andrew, to millions throughout the world, was to be a voluble child and a bright, uninhibited woman.

As she cried lustily in her mother's arms, the new baby's future mother-in-law, Queen Elizabeth II was five months pregnant with Prince Andrew, her third child and second son.

Both Sarah and Andrew, who arrived within four months of each other, would one day help to create a new dimension in the variegated personality of the royal family. Their births coincided with a time of change in public attitude towards royalty, which in turn brought change for the royal family itself. For by 1960, as the Queen's reign neared the end of its first decade, it had become fashionable to decry the monarchy. Vociferous criticism, mainly from Lord Altrincham (now John Grigg), Malcolm Muggeridge, John Osborne and Willie Hamilton, MP, centred on the Queen's old-fashioned establishment at the Palace.

'My objection to the Royal symbol,' said John Osborne in 1956 in his play *Look Back in Anger*, 'is that it is dead; it is a gold filling in a mouth full of decay.' In 1957 Malcolm Muggeridge sardonically referred to the doings

A study of the young Sarah Ferguson at Lowood

of the British royal family as 'the royal soap opera'.

Amongst those urging a rethink was the Queen's own husband, Philip, Duke of Edinburgh. Unlike most of the Queen's advisors, he did not dismiss the critics lightly, but urged his wife 'to take account' of their views. He had suffered from the over-bearing domination of the old-style courtiers himself.

So, gradually the old staff were weeded out to be replaced by the new Queen's men. The Court became more flexible, adapting to contemporary values but still maintaining the principles the Queen had grown up with – namely the secure foundations of family life. These monarchial changes affected the Queen's outlook on life. Who, for instance, on the day Prince Andrew was born, could have foreseen that twenty-six years later his mother would readily and happily give her blessing to a match with a commoner whose past, moreover, included two well-documented love affairs?

When the Princess of Wales became engaged she was not only a virgin but officially declared to be one. To her considerable embarrassment, her uncle Lord Fermoy

With her mother, driving an imaginary car

told a group of journalists: 'Lady Diana, I can assure you, has never had a lover. There is no such thing as her ever having a past.'

Sarah's less than snow-white past was received without question by her future mother-in-law, whose eyes and mind had long become accustomed to the ways of the world. Accepting the two close relationships in Sarah's recent past, the Queen looked instead towards the contribution this bouncy, 'gutsy' young woman would bring to a royal family poised on the threshold of the twenty-first century.

'She is a thoroughly modern woman,' commented the *Daily Express*. 'She'll be a thoroughly modern wife.' More significantly, Sarah was the woman Prince Andrew loved, and of course the Queen wanted him to be happy.

When Malcolm Muggeridge coined the now familiar phrase 'the royal soap opera', he could not have envisaged the 'show-biz' razmatazz that Diana, Princess of Wales, who quickly became well established as a 'megastar' in the royal firmament, would inspire almost thirty years later. Nor could he have guessed that the doings of the royal family would in the 1980s come to be known by the media as 'The Palace Dallas'.

A family snap of the young Sarah (right)

The TATLER
& BYSTANDER

JAN. 16, 1957
TWO SHILLINGS

MRS RONALD FERGUSON

Sarah's mother gracing the cover of The Tatler, *January 1957*

Sarah (left) with her sister Jane

It is interesting to compare the popular attitude of the 1960s with that of the 1980s. Enchantment with the royal family has surely never been greater. The marriage of the Prince and Princess of Wales in 1981 dramatically illustrated that point. The occasion of the Queen's sixtieth birthday, in April 1986, was another much-publicized celebration. *The Times* noted on the day that she was 'one who adapted the monarchy to the times and maintained it, proving that the institution still had some value'. Then came the wedding of Prince Andrew – another event welcomed by the British public. The critics have surely been proved wrong.

Astride her first pony

Sarah's grandmother, Lady Elmhirst

A potential superstar in her own right, Sarah Margaret Ferguson is the latest in a long line of royal brides to capture the nation's imagination. With the Prince and Princess of Wales, she and Prince Andrew represent a close-knit, unbeatable and very British team, with a modern, fresh approach that should clear away the last traces of Hanoverian fustiness.

Unaware of her younger daughter's destiny, Susan Ferguson took her home to Lowood, the family's large, comfortable house, at Sunninghill, Ascot, just a few miles from Windsor Castle. There toddler Jane, the elder daughter (now Mrs William Makim), waited to welcome her new sister to the light, sunny nursery. Sarah's father was then in the regular army. He is now Prince Charles's polo manager and runs the Guards' Polo Club at Windsor.

Sarah grew into a lively child with the distinctive Celtic colouring of her Irish-Scottish origins. Her paternal grandmother, Lady Elmhirst, was a Montagu-Douglas-Scott, the family name of the Buccleuchs. She married first Colonel Andrew Ferguson, Sarah's grandfather, and then, after his death, Air Marshal Sir Thomas Elmhirst who died in 1966.

Sarah's grandmother, whom Sarah closely resembles, lives today in a cottage near Dummer Down House in Hampshire, close to the Ferguson family home. She is a first cousin of Princess Alice, Duchess of Gloucester, whose father was the seventh Duke of Buccleuch. The present Duke, in his youth, had the same red hair and freckles as Sarah.

Unlike the Princess of Wales, who was 'a prim and rather proper little girl' according to her biographer Anthony Holden, Sarah was always bright and pushy; 'an outgoing child who brought me a lot of happiness,' says her father. Her first encounter with the royal family came when her father was in the Life Guards and the Ferguson girls were given the freedom of the gardens at Windsor. They used to go to watch polo at Smith's Lawn when their father was playing. Here they met the

With her mother and sister

Major Ronald Ferguson in polo gear

(Right) Father of the bride: 'Major Ronald' relaxing at Smith's Lawn, Windsor

royal children who had come to watch their own father play.

According to Sarah's mother, now Mrs Hector Bar-rantes, she and Andrew met behind the pony lines on the polo field at Windsor. Mrs Barrantes said, in her amusing, understated way: 'Doesn't everyone [meet like that]?' – thus underlining the tight little charmed circle around the throne into which Sarah was born.

One of Sarah's earliest memories (and this is some-thing Andrew also experienced) is of playing at the end of a cord attached to her waist held by a grown-up so that she did not stray on to the polo field while her father – as Prince Andrew recalled on his engagement day – thundered by.

At that time, Major Ferguson was Commander of the Sovereign's Escort of the Household Cavalry, the fourth generation of his family to serve in the Life Guards, and one of the Duke of Edinburgh's small circle of male friends, mainly because of their shared passion

for polo. 'Polo stick-in-waiting,' the Queen dubbed the tall, dashing cavalryman; he was always known as 'Major Ronald' to the royal children.

Both the Queen and Prince Philip liked him. They were as distressed as all his friends when, soon after Sarah's thirteenth birthday, her mother left the family home, eventually to marry Argentinian polo-player Hector Barrantes. They, too, had met on the polo field.

It was a meeting that was to bring much heartache to Sarah and her sister Jane who were to grow up without a mother's presence in their home. 'Of course it affected her. But I don't think it changed her,' said Major Ferguson. Naturally unhappy after the departure of her mother to faraway Argentina with Mr Barrantes, Sarah clung to her father who gave her the stability and strength of mind that is so important a facet of her personality today. Although she favours her father in looks, Sarah gets her happy, bouncy nature from her mother.

Sarah's father with his second wife, Susan

Her father eventually married again in 1976 and gave his daughters a much-loved step-mother. She was Susan Deptford, a Norfolk farmer's daughter. Her description of the way Sarah welcomed her into the family gives an insight into Sarah's personality. 'She was very close to her real mother, but she went out of her way to make me feel welcome and was enthusiastic about me becoming part of the family,' says Mrs Ferguson. 'Her personality is a very happy one. She would never melt into the back-ground. She was just the same at fourteen as she is now.'

Sarah, like her new sister-in-law (and fourth cousin) the Princess of Wales – whose own mother left home when she was a child – was sent away to boarding school in an attempt to bridge the vulnerable years of her early teens. Before her mother left Sarah had been a pupil at Mrs Latham's School, Englefield Green, and Daneshill, a co-ed preparatory school. Now she was sent to Hurst

Sarah's mother with her second husband, Hector Barrantes

Daneshill School, near Sarah's home

The school where Sarah became Head Girl

Dummer Down House in Hampshire

Sarah Ferguson as a schoolgirl, centre back row

Lodge, Sunningdale – a school for girls up to the fifth year with approximately 200 pupils, about a third of whom are boarders. Yet she is obviously not the sort of person who remains depressed for long. Although initially insecure, Sarah's irrepressible nature soon reappeared and she did well at school, and she ended up being joint headgirl.

'Sarah was a particularly charming person with a very bubbly personality. She made a very good headgirl,' a member of the staff recalls.

Fenella Heron, daughter of comedian Ted Rodgers, now married herself and the mother of a toddler, was Fergie's joint headgirl. 'I'm very proud of her,' she says.

Another former school friend Alexandra Grant-

Jane's wedding, 1976, at which Sarah was bridesmaid, aged sixteen

great enthusiasm as her step-mother. I don't know how I'd have coped if she hadn't.'

Sarah now has a half-brother Andrew, aged seven, who was a page at her wedding, and two half-sisters – Alice, five, who was a bridesmaid, and the baby, Eliza, to whom Prince Charles is god-father.

When she left school in 1976 with six 'O' levels – in Art, English Language and Literature, Spoken English,

Adamson, now a nurse, remembered those noisy, rumbustious school days. 'Fergie was always well to the fore. She was very boisterous,' she said. Another, Lisa Mulidore, now an actress, describes Sarah as very popular. 'On school open days I always remember Fergie surrounded by younger pupils. They hero-worshipped her.'

Said yet another old friend: 'She is particularly loyal and always takes a balanced view. She thinks things out.'

The young Sarah was always full of mischief, as she is now. Says Fenella Heron: 'When I saw her poking fun at the Prince during their engagement interview I knew she hadn't changed a bit.'

According to another friend: 'Fergie used to egg us on, and if we were up to something we shouldn't have been, then Fergie was always the leader.'

Susan Ferguson, whom Sarah jokingly calls 'my wicked step-mother', commented: 'People just relax in her company because her laughter makes them feel at ease.'

Susan Ferguson speaks warmly of that time: 'It says much for Fergie's big heart that she welcomed me with

French and Biology – she went out to Argentina to spend a holiday with her mother and step-father. By this time, old wounds had healed between her parents. Major Ferguson today emphasizes their cordial relationship: 'Susan [Barrantes] and I see each other every year when she comes to England to see her family. I think the media prefers to think that we both hate each other, but our relationship has been very civilized, and that goes for her new husband as well.'

Sarah had a wonderful holiday in Argentina – riding, swimming and catching up on all the lost years when she and her mother had been apart. She got on well with

Susan Ferguson with her children at Dummer Down House

A Ferguson family group, Sarah with her father, sister Jane and nephew Seamus

Sarah with her baby half-sister Eliza

Polo at Windsor. Sarah with Laura Smith-Bingham, 1979

her step-father and also met a young man who was to be important in her life for a short time when they remet three years later. He was Kim Smith-Bingham, an old Etonian, who had taken a job on a neighbouring ranch. By coincidence, his sister Laura had been at school with Sarah.

Meanwhile, at her mother's suggestion, Sarah took a nine-months' secretarial course at Queen's College, Kensington.

'A bright, bouncy red-head,' was the written assessment of her when she left. 'A bit slap-dash, but has initiative and personality which she will use well to her advantage when she gets older and accepts responsibility happily.'

Like most girls at seventeen, however, Sarah was not ready to settle down in a steady job. She dabbled with several, working first for a flat-letting agency and then an art dealer. But it was while employed with a public relations agency, Durden-Smith Communications, that she learnt some of her most valuable lessons; particularly noticeable with the media during the weeks that led up to her engagement to Prince Andrew when she was very much in the public eye.

One of the friends she had met at secretarial college was Charlotte Eden, daughter of Lord Eden, who partnered her on an adventure holiday to South America soon after her twenty-first birthday.

They travelled thousands of miles by bus, once sleeping in a scruffy shelter at Iguazu Falls on the border between Argentina, Paraguay and Brazil. 'It was pretty rough,' Charlotte has recalled. 'We used a guide book and tried to find all the cheapie places to stay. We had our bus and air tickets, of course, but by the time we got off the bus at Iguazu Falls we'd run out of money. So we slept at the bus station on the benches. The next morning we were hungry but we knew what to do.'

In South America they always put down a small plate of cheese when a drink is ordered. 'So trying to look as prosperous as possible, we sauntered into a nearby hotel and asked for two glasses of water. They brought the water and put down the cheese. We scoffed the lot.'

Sarah remet Kim Smith-Bingham, who became her first love, when she went to Verbier in Switzerland on holiday from her public relations job. He was selling ski-wear in a fashionable boutique to which Sarah was taken by Kim's sister Laura.

Although married now with a small daughter, Kim is still a good friend of Sarah's. 'We never "lived together" as the papers said, but we did spend a lot of time together,' he recalls. 'Sarah would ski every day while I was working. She is very good, black run standard.'

He describes Sarah as a good cook who loved giving small dinner parties. 'She is a marvellous hostess. People say that red-heads have a terrible temper. Sarah didn't. All I can say about her was she was not a typical red-head.'

'My wife Fiona and I still see a lot of Fergie. We're still in the same set and good friends,' Kim says.

With the exit of Kim the stage was set for Paddy McNally, a widower with two young sons. He was twenty-two years older than Sarah and was formerly racing manager to Niki Lauda.

Life with Paddy, as Sarah was to find, was always in the fast lane. He moved in a sophisticated international set unlike any she had known. These jetsetting, cosmopolitan women were very different to the 'Sloane-type' girls with whom she had grown up. The men were mainly fast-drinking, cosmopolitan and abrasive. Sarah's family were deeply worried by her relationship with McNally. Although they liked him, it was felt that the gap in their ages was too great; as one of the Ferguson

Kim Smith-Bingham

Sarah with Paddy McNally

had always liked the relaxed, spontaneous daughter of her husband's polo manager. Earlier she had wanted her as a lady-in-waiting but Sarah had just met McNally and the time was not right.

Now, sensing her unhappiness at the imminent break-up of her love affair, Diana suggested that Sarah might be invited to join the Queen's Ascot week house-party at Windsor Castle when the royal family holds open house to personal friends. It was June 1985.

Prince Andrew was home on leave from the Navy and, as his sister-in-law knew, he was still feeling the after-effects of his romance with Koo Stark, the actress, who had been his first really serious love. Fortune smiled and he was instantly attracted to the lively young woman with the flame-coloured hair whom his sister-in-law had chosen as a likely Ascot partner for him.

friends put it: 'Of course her father was concerned. What father would approve of his daughter going out with a man almost his own age?'

Towards the end of their relationship, feelings were as fraught as they usually are when a parting seems imminent. They had one last holiday together in Majorca and then gradually edged out of each other's lives.

In Switzerland Sarah had met a British businessman, Richard Burton, who was based in Geneva. He offered her a job as London representative of his publishing company, BCK Graphic Arts, with an office in St George's Street, Hanover Square, in central London. The job involved liaising with authors and photographers, a role she plans to continue after her marriage. Said Burton: 'Fergie is wonderful at handling people, especially entertaining them, which is part of her job. It does not require a vast knowledge of art. It's more a matter of common sense, and she has lots of that.'

With her reappearance in London, Sarah began to see a lot of her old friend, the Princess of Wales, who

The dashing prince arrives

Ascot 1985: Prince Andrew and Sarah leave the Royal Enclosure

Back in 1970 at Smith's Lawn, Windsor, Andrew had teased Sarah unmercifully about her red hair and freckles. 'Carrots!' he used to jeer. A Ferguson family friend remembers there then ensued a 'battle-royal' between the two ten year-olds and Sarah 'gave as good as she got'.

The same sort of horseplay, if slightly more restrained, amused the Queen and other members of the royal family in the royal box at Ascot race-course on 20 June. It was the first 'grown-up' meeting of Sarah and Andrew, and he tried to 'force-feed' her chocolate profiteroles. 'I'm on a diet,' she retorted, dodging the sticky confection

and, in the process, landing a not-so-playful right-hander at the Prince. The Queen, it was reported, was delighted her second son had, as she put it, 'met his match'.

Prince Andrew then returned to his ship and Sarah went off to Majorca for a last holiday with McNally. In late October when Andrew had some leave they started going out together. At that time Sarah was sharing a flat in Lavender Gardens, Clapham Junction, in south-west London, with Carolyn Beckwith-Smith, whose cousin Anne is principal lady-in-waiting to the Princess of Wales.

Carolyn was engaged to an old Etonian Harry Cot-

Carolyn Beckwith-Smith, now Mrs Harry Cotterell

Lavender Gardens, Clapham Junction

terell, and the two girls shared dinner parties, through the autumn and early winter months as the romance between Sarah and Andrew became more serious. Before long, neighbours noticed a dark-green Jaguar parked outside the flat with a man inside and were worried the street was being observed prior to a burglary. In the end, the word got around that the occupant of the car was Prince Andrew's long-suffering detective. Later, conscious that others in the street were being disturbed by journalists and photographers, Sarah even invited

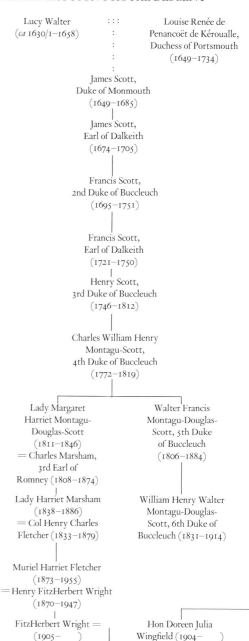

SARAH FERGUSON'S ROYAL DESCENT

Lucy Walter		Louise Renée de
(ca 1630/1–1658)	:::	Penancoët de Kéroualle,
	:	Duchess of Portsmouth
	:	(1649–1734)

James Scott,
Duke of Monmouth
(1649–1685)

James Scott,
Earl of Dalkeith
(1674–1705)

Francis Scott,
2nd Duke of Buccleuch
(1695–1751)

Francis Scott,
Earl of Dalkeith
(1721–1750)

Henry Scott,
3rd Duke of Buccleuch
(1746–1812)

Charles William Henry
Montagu-Scott,
4th Duke of Buccleuch
(1772–1819)

Lady Margaret	Walter Francis
Harriet Montagu-	Montagu-Douglas-
Douglas-Scott	Scott, 5th Duke
(1811–1846)	of Buccleuch
= Charles Marsham,	(1806–1884)
3rd Earl of	
Romney (1808–1874)	
Lady Harriet Marsham	William Henry Walter
(1838–1886)	Montagu-Douglas-
= Col Henry Charles	Scott, 6th Duke of
Fletcher (1833–1879)	Buccleuch (1831–1914)

Muriel Harriet Fletcher
(1873–1955)
= Henry FitzHerbert Wright
(1870–1947)

| FitzHerbert Wright = | Hon Doreen Julia |
| (1905–   ) | Wingfield (1904–   ) |

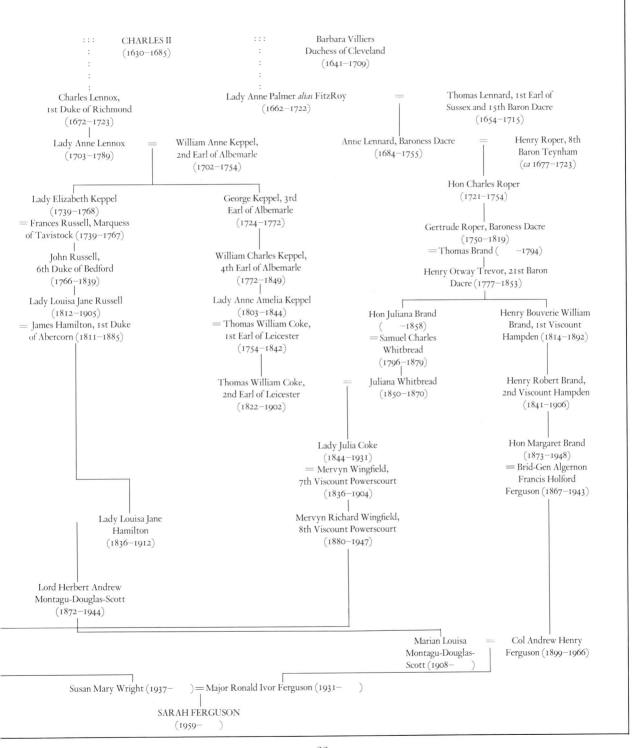

her next-door neighbour in to meet Andrew, who offered apologies that he had been worried by Press questioning.

The frigate HMS *Brazen* with helicopter pilot Andrew aboard was based in Devonport, near Plymouth, for a month from 18 December 1985, so the couple saw a lot of each other during that time. Indeed, by Christmas Major Ferguson described the relationship as 'strong', but denied they were engaged. The two spent the holiday with their respective families – Andrew at Windsor and Sarah not far away in Hampshire.

At New Year Andrew asked the Queen to invite Sarah to Sandringham, just as Charles did with Diana in the last stages of their courtship. Now it was obvious to everyone that this was not just another of Andrew's 'affairs'. On 20 January 1986 he rejoined *Brazen* and sailed to Gothenburg in Sweden before returning to London the following month.

'Fergie' still smiling despite the attentions of press photographers

Sarah Ferguson ski-ing in Klosters, Switzerland, 1986

Sarah with her father at Dummer Down Farm. (Right) In an outfit borrowed from the Princess of Wales, Sarah visits HMS Brazen, *February 1986*

Sarah, in the meantime, had returned from Hampshire and discovered her flat in a virtual state of siege. The 'rat-pack' or 'The Lavender Hill Mob', as she called the journalists and photographers assembled there, were now camping more or less permanently on her doorstep.

Jayne Fincher, the award-winning royal photographer and veteran of the Diana–Charles engagement, testifies to Sarah's unfailing good humour and courtesy during a very trying time. 'A lovely person – we gave her full marks,' she says.

As the media alternated between praising or dissecting her, Sarah's public relations training helped her to remain unruffled and smiling.

'The primitive ritual of transforming an ordinary girl into a Princess,' enthused the *Sunday Telegraph*; 'Has much more in the melons department than Koo Stark,' proclaimed the *Sun*, noted for its more basic observations; 'Randy Andy finds a Dandy,' said the *New York Daily News*.

By now, Sarah was wearing on her little finger one of her Christmas presents from Andrew; a triple Russian wedding ring of gold, just like the one Prince Charles gave to Diana Spencer. It is said to be a pre-engagement symbol in Sloane-land.

In early February 1986 the Prince was in London for a four-day courtesy visit by HMS *Brazen* and invited the Princess of Wales and her son William to come aboard. 'Why don't you bring Sarah?' he suggested. Immediately word got out, and what had been planned as a private visit became extremely public. Hemmed in by photographers, Diana urged her future sister-in-law to 'keep smiling'. She also lent her a black and white check outfit for the occasion.

Brazen took part in NATO exercises with Andrew flying his helicopter 'Brazen Hussey', as Sarah joined the Prince and Princess of Wales for a skiing holiday at Klosters in Switzerland.

In Fleet Street speculation by now had reached fever-pitch. Everywhere Sarah went she found photographers, and outwitting them was no easy task. Nevertheless, her time in the international racing circuit had made her a brilliant driver. 'Fierce,' said one photographer who'd been defeated by Sarah's fearless handling of her blue BMW through the dense London traffic.

'Fergie'

(Right) Floors Castle, where Andrew proposed to Sarah

'She was laughing most of the time. I believe she really enjoyed it – especially as I lost her and she had the last laugh,' he said.

On another occasion, Sarah popped into Sotheby's, hotly pursued by the *paparazzi* who waited for her to re-appear. Little did they realize that she had disappeared into the warren of underground rooms and had emerged on the other side of the building!

Prince Andrew was away at sea for his twenty-sixth birthday on 19 February 1986 but three days later Sarah

flew north, using the name 'Miss Anwell' on the passenger list, to meet him secretly at Floors Castle, the vast turreted home on the Scottish borders of the Duke and Duchess of Roxburghe.

The wind howled and the rain swirled round the Castle as the couple dined with the Duke and Duchess. After dinner they retired to the drawing-room to sit by the blazing log fire. It is a magnificent room, painted pale Adam green with wall panels outlined in gold. There are two large pale green sofas on each side of the fireplace, and the walls are hung with fine Belgian tapestries. It was here (their host and hostess having pleaded an early night) that Sarah and Andrew decided to marry.

In that romantic setting – and down 'on both knees' – Prince Andrew proposed. Sarah laughingly accepted but told him, 'When you wake up tomorrow morning you can tell me that it's all a huge joke.' He didn't but then followed yet another long difficult month until, at 10 a.m. on 19 March the formal announcement confirming the couple's engagement was released by Buckingham Palace. Delighted though they were, the Press loudly proclaimed it to be, 'the worst-kept secret of the year'.

The drawing-room at Floors Castle. (Right) Sarah leaving the Royal College of Arms

ANDREW

Like the rest of his family, Prince Andrew appears totally at ease in the glaring royal spotlight. Handsome and trendy he epitomizes a dashing, media prince.

But the private man can be very different. He shows promise of becoming a 'fireside and slippers' family figure; the sort who will be most content with a comfortable, happy soul like Sarah who, nevertheless, has more than a dash of spark and passion beneath that jolly, sporty exterior.

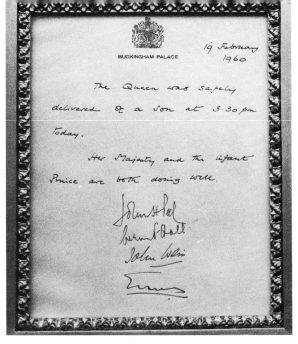

The handwritten announcement of Prince Andrew's birth

When Prince Andrew returned home from active service in the Falklands campaign in 1982 – the first royal prince of his generation to experience battle – he revealed in a few terse words how much being treated as any other serviceman, with no royal privileges, had meant to him.

'I am not going back to be a prince. I am a pilot not a prince,' he said.

It was said lightly but with evident determination and, as the Queen's second son, now fourth in line to the throne, Prince Andrew has a good chance of realizing this ambition. Between him and the throne are his elder brother, the Prince of Wales, and his two healthy nephews, William and Harry. With every addition to the Wales family, Andrew is nudged further down the line – a situation he has made clear does not displease him.

When Prince William was born on 21 June 1982, his uncle was aboard his ship, the aircraft carrier HMS *Invincible*, in Falkland waters. His excitement was infectious when the signal came through and, as he ordered drinks all round, someone asked him why he was so pleased to

Royal Salute from the Tower of London

be pushed out of the immediate line of succession. 'I'm absolutely delighted,' replied Prince Andrew. 'Now I have a chance of a bit more privacy.'

Although he appears at ease in the public spotlight, Andrew much prefers to be out of it and for most of his life has enjoyed a more relaxed life-style than the rest of his family.

He was born in the ground-floor Belgian Suite at Buckingham Palace on 19 February 1960. This suite is normally only used for important state visitors but was preferred by the Queen on this occasion because her own room was far too noisy due to the crowds outside the Palace. From his birth Prince Andrew – as is often the way with the younger children in a family – was treated in a more emancipated manner than the Queen's elder pair, Charles and Anne, although his arrival was marked with much pomp and ceremony.

At half-past three in the afternoon, thirty-six Hunter jets of the Black Arrows performed a fly-past over London. There were loyal addresses in Parliament, 21-gun salutes in Hyde Park, the Tower of London and Windsor Castle. Around Buckingham Palace and in the Mall crowds were tightly packed – dark masses against a background of flags and bunting.

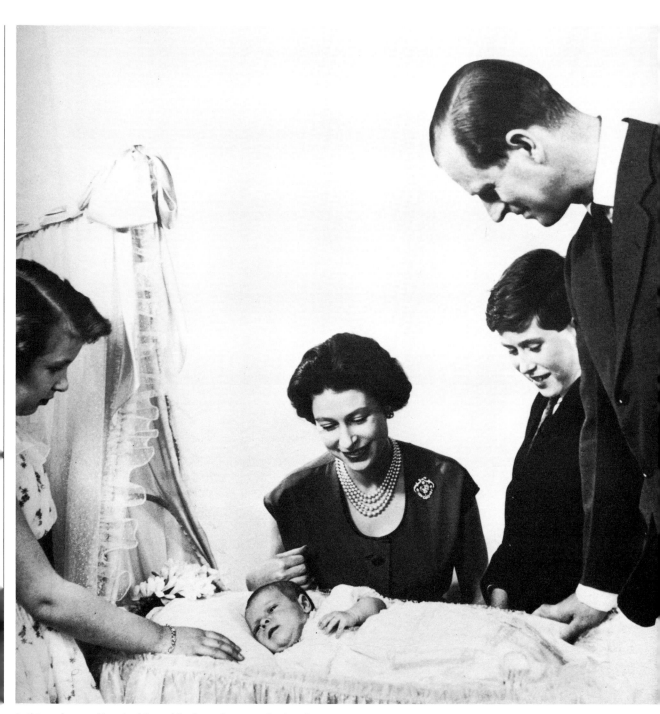

Cecil Beaton's memorable study of the royal family round Prince Andrew's cradle

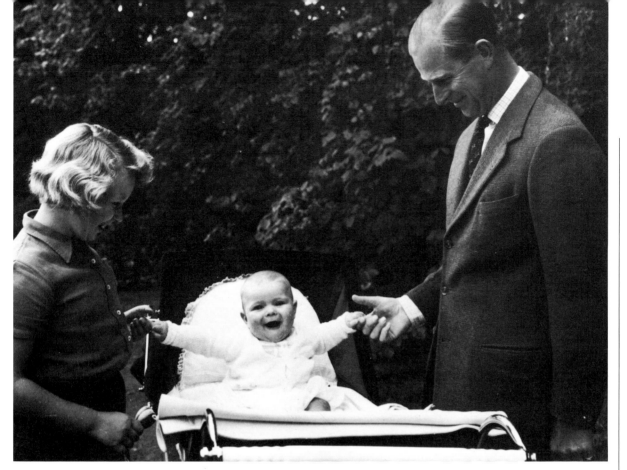

With Princess Anne and Prince Philip. (Left) The Prince with his grandmother on Queen Elizabeth's sixtieth birthday, 4 August 1960

The Queen got on with state business, sitting up in bed and reading her 'boxes' a few hours after Andrew was born. He weighed 7 lb. 3 ounces, had light brown hair and his mother's fine blue eyes. His loving family surrounded him from the beginning as they gathered round his cot to admire the latest addition to their royal ranks. The Duke of Edinburgh rushed from his study when he heard the news, collected Princess Anne from the schoolroom and took her to visit her new brother within half an hour of his birth.

Prince Andrew was the first infant born to a reigning sovereign since the days of Queen Victoria. Four doctors, headed by Lord Evans and assisted by Sister Helen Rowe, were present at his arrival. But, as with Prince Charles and Princess Anne, the Queen did not invite the Home Secretary, as had previously been the custom, to be present at the confinement.

Prince Charles, then aged twelve, was telephoned at Cheam school, where he was a boarder, and a notice was pinned to the Palace gates: 'The Queen was safely delivered of a son at 3.30 p.m. today. Her Majesty and the infant prince are both doing well.'

Later that evening the Queen Mother and Princess Margaret arrived, closely followed by Princess Marina, Duchess of Kent and her daughter Princess Alexandra, who was to be Andrew's god-mother.

For his christening in the music room at Buckingham Palace on 8 April 1960, the ritual adopted for all royal babies since Queen Victoria's brood was followed. The silver gilt font, designed by Prince Albert, Andrew's great-great-great-grandfather, arrived from Windsor. The fragile Honiton lace christening robe first worn in 1842 by his great-great-grandfather, the future Edward VII, was gently eased onto the chubby baby.

Face at the nursery window

A few days before his birth the Queen, in a royal decree, had changed her children's surname from Windsor to Mountbatten-Windsor, in an acknowledgement of her husband's dynasty. Now two months later, the infant was named Andrew, after the Duke of Edinburgh's father; Albert after the Queen's father; Christian after King Christian of Denmark, his paternal great-great-grandfather; and Edward after Edward VII, his maternal great-great-grandfather.

Once more the old Palace nursery, that had seen so many royal children, had an occupant. Princess Anne, aged ten when he was born, spent most of her time away from the schoolroom, there helping Mabel Anderson whom she was eventually to employ as nanny to her own young son, the Queen's first grandson, Peter Phillips, born on 15 November 1977.

Both tender and protective towards her little brother, Anne could hardly be dragged away from pram-pushing duties long enough to be measured for the dress she wore as bridesmaid to her aunt, Princess Margaret, when she married Antony Armstrong-Jones in Westminster Abbey on 6 May 1960. (A marriage that was dissolved in May 1978.)

The Queen, too, spent as much time as possible with Andrew — dashing upstairs to don the rubber apron she kept there for bathtime. Often distinguished family visitors from overseas found themselves giving a helping hand to bath the young prince. Once he had several members of a European royal house scrubbing his back and sailing his rubber boats.

The Queen herself was fulfilled, and it showed in a new, relaxed awareness. She thoroughly enjoyed her baby son and they have always been particularly close. She has never been regarded as a cuddly person — but Andrew cuddled her then and still cuddles her today, reducing her to helpless laughter by tickling her when he thinks he can get away with it.

She was to spend more time with this baby than with her first two children — even allowing him to play as she worked in her study, which had always been banned to Charles and Anne when they were small. Toys were

With the Queen after Trooping the Colour, 1962

On the East Terrace at Windsor Castle. The Queen holds on to her son as he investigates the fountain's pool

kept in a drawer of her desk, and young Andrew played contentedly as his mother dealt with weighty matters pertaining to state and country. Andrew, unlike his brother Charles, was unlikely ever to be concerned with such things. The Queen spent every available moment with Andrew and he, according to his nurse, Scots-born Mabel Anderson, was from the first, 'placid, content and full of fun'.

On the balcony of Buckingham Palace after Trooping the Colour: Lord Mountbatten, Princess Margaret, the Queen Mother, Viscount Linley and Prince Andrew, watch the approach of saluting aircraft

When the Queen was preparing for a tour of India and Pakistan, in 1961, she was so miserable at the prospect of being separated from toddler Andrew that Princess Anne came up with the plan to send a weekly batch of photographs taken by herself with her new camera.

Andrew was a fortunate baby, surrounded by love. 'Full of smiles' and 'wonderful in every respect', said Sister Helen Rowe who helped to bring him into the world. All the old toys came out, and more of his own helped to clutter the big glass-fronted cupboards in the nursery. For Andrew's second birthday, Charles, then fourteen, made him a pink wooden rocking elephant. Soon after that his mother gave him his first riding lessons on a Shetland pony called Dinkum.

Because he was an 'only' child (in the sense that his brother and sister were much older), the Queen used to ask other children to come to the Palace several times a week. Andrew's two cousins, David, Viscount Linley, Princess Margaret's son born on 3 November 1961, and George, Earl of St Andrews, son of the Duke of Kent

The royal family in the grounds of Frogmore House, near Windsor Castle, spring 1965

Prince Andrew with his brother Edward in the Palace garden

born on 26 June 1962, were among those who came to play when they were old enough.

This much-loved small boy grew up, inevitably, rather spoilt, although in due course he had a younger brother Edward, born on 10 March 1964, to share the attention of his mother, sister and nurses. Andrew, now four, graduated to lessons in the schoolroom with Miss Kathleen Peebles, nicknamed 'Mispy' (Miss P) by Charles and Anne.

Already the Queen had given Andrew his first simple Bible lessons and taught him the alphabet. Now, with several children of the Queen's friends, including his great favourite Katie Seymour of the brewing family

with whom he spent seaside holidays on the Isle of Wight, Andrew began his first real lessons.

Prince Philip, as he did with the other children, took over the sporting side of his education. He taught him to swim in the Palace pool and showed him how to box. Once the Duke turned up at an evening engagement sporting a black eye after an over-enthusiastic bout with Andrew. Later the young prince had private tennis coaching with Dan Maskell and cricket coaching with Ken Mincer. When he was older Graham Hill taught him to drive.

He was, above all, treated firstly as a normal child and secondly as a prince. On occasions his behaviour caused his mother to remark he was 'a bit of a handful'.

Prince Andrew at Braemar

He could be quite stubborn at times. Refusing to wear tartan shorts under his kilt because, he said: 'Papa doesn't wear them.'

Escapades, as he grew older, included the much-quoted tying together of a guardsman's bootlaces. Then there was a bubble-bath episode in the Windsor fountains, closely followed by emptying washing-up liquid from the nursery kitchen in the Palace swimming pool. This was accounted a rather more serious matter as the bubbles reached the ceiling and were only discovered because water flowed out to the terrace outside.

Other noteworthy and punishable 'offences' including shinning up the scaffolding at Windsor Castle when restoration work was underway; placing a 'whoopee' cushion under an embarrassed Anglican bishop at Balmoral and driving his 'James Bond' pedal car into his mother's corgi pack. The car had been a present from his parents for his sixth birthday. It was complete with artificial machine guns and a smoke system and cost a reputed £4,000 to build. It still stands in a passage at Buckingham Palace, waiting for young visitors like Peter Phillips.

At Smith's Lawn, between chukkas

53

Prince Andrew takes charge of his mother's corgis at Windsor. With him are Lady Sarah Armstrong-Jones, Princess Margaret, the Queen Mother, the Queen and Lord Linley (obscured)

The Queen and Prince Andrew at the Braemar Games, 1966

The royal family at Sandringham, 1968

As a boisterous wolf cub

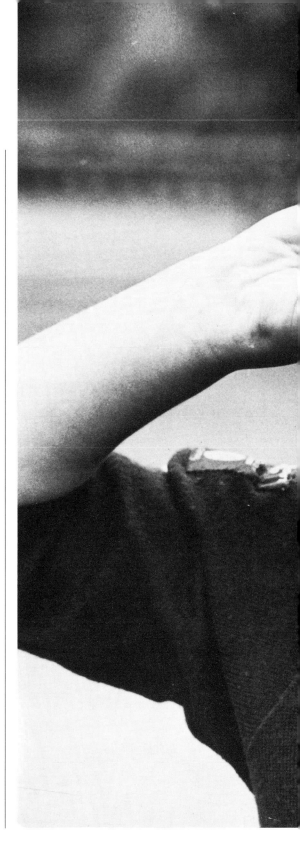

They were all predictably normal misdemeanours which would have been fair game for most lively youngsters fortunate enough to have at hand a sentry, fountain, swimming pool, Bishop or corgi pack. Certainly Andrew's antics brought some light relief to the royal household, if only to wonder what he would be up to next.

Some of his energy was channelled into being an enthusiastic Wolf Cub, and every week a mini-bus arrived at the Palace bringing the other members of the 1st Marylebone Wolf Cub Pack. Their backgrounds were mixed and their reactions to the extremely grand setting for their meetings ranged from awe to complete nonchalance.

In September 1968, the term before his ninth birth-

On holiday in the Isle of Wight. Prince Andrew loved sailing even in his childhood

Andrew and Sarah: an early informal study at Windsor

day, the Queen and the Duke of Edinburgh took him to Heatherdown Preparatory School, not far from Windsor Castle, to begin life as a boarder.

He shared a dormitory with six other boys and often took friends back to the Castle for a slap-up tea at weekends. His birthday cakes, made by the royal chef, and usually featuring a rugby game or ships, were especially popular as they were always big enough for the whole school.

His schoolfriends remember Andrew as being a generous boy, always prepared to share any of his possessions. He achieved a certain reputation for pranks and one of his more memorable exploits was to shin up the school flag-pole for a dare and leave his shirt flying in the brisk wind.

By this time, Andrew was quite friendly with a certain red-headed schoolgirl called Sarah, who was usually to be found at Smith's Lawn during summer holiday weekends. They helped form a small gang of polo players' children who congregated behind the pony lines or 'galloped' around playing noisy games. They took it in turns to be the gangleader.

When he was thirteen, Andrew was sent to Gordonstoun school in Morayshire in the footsteps of his father and brother. There he settled down extremely well under

In a rugby scrum at Heatherdown: Prince Andrew, centre

With his mother and cousin David Linley at Badminton

the spartan conditions which the Duke of Edinburgh –
who had experienced them himself – considered so
necessary in the upbringing of his sons.

Charles reportedly hated Gordonstoun, but his two
younger brothers enjoyed it. By their time conditions
were much easier and the school was co-educational,
which certainly added to its appeal as far as Andrew
was concerned.

True to the form he was to show in all his pre-marital
years, he gathered around him the most attractive girls
in the school who became known as 'Andy's Harem'.
His nickname 'Randy Andy' dates from these days.

This tag followed him to the 1976 Olympics in
Montreal, when he accompanied his parents and saw
his sister Princess Anne ride with the British Equestrian
Team. It was then, at the age of sixteen, he first fell
under the spell of Canada. There, too, the 'glamour boy'
reputation took root and was to stay with him certainly
until his marriage.

'If they'd handed out medals for sex appeal Britain
would have cake-walked it,' wrote one woman's magazine

An attractive companion for the teenaged Prince

at the time, 'and the recipient would have been Prince
Andrew.'

His official companion on that trip was blonde Sandi
Jones, daughter of the Director-General of Olympic
yachting events, Colonel Campbell Jones. She was later
to become quite a regular girl-friend when the Prince
attended Lakefield College, seventy miles from Toronto,
while participating in a pupil exchange from Gordonstoun.

Sandi revealed some of the difficulties experienced
with a royal boy-friend. 'There wasn't much romancing
under the eye of Andrew's bodyguards – though we man-

With Carolyn Beckwith-Smith

The Prince canoeing in Canada

aged to give them the slip on occasions. He is just an ordinary guy who wants to have fun with a girl-friend.'

Andrew also achieved something of a reputation as a sportsman in Canada, even earning a tribute about his ice-hockey from the Lakefield head boy David Miller: 'He was pretty good. He was quite vicious and you have to be a bit vicious to be good at this game.'

When he got into the 1st Rugby XV Andrew was cheered on by girls in T-shirts proclaiming: 'I'm an Andy Windsor girl' – a story that amused his mother.

Before he left Canada, Andrew was writing home about wind-surfing, canoeing and bob-sleighing. One memorable trip on which he kept a diary for his parents was a 200-mile journey down Coppermine River to the Arctic Ocean by canoe, shooting the rapids among other adventures. Often Andrew's letters from Canada became quite dog-eared as the Queen passed them round the family.

Back at Gordonstoun, he captained the cricket XI and gained a 'gold' in the Duke of Edinburgh's Award

Scheme. He was captain of his house but never school captain like his father and two brothers.

During his last year at school he managed some incognito trips, usually travelling as Andrew Cambridge. He went to France and Germany to improve his languages, and sailed the Gordonstoun ketch round Scotland in stormy weather with other seniors.

Andrew always loved the sea, and Gordonstoun, situated so near the Moray Firth, helped to encourage this leaning towards a nautical life. His father had taught him to sail his own aluminium craft on Loch Muich, beneath the shadow of Lochnagar mountain. At school he helped man a coastguard watch tower and their own in-shore rescue team.

Prince Andrew with his younger brother Edward

At Gordonstoun, too, Andrew had his first flying lessons. At fifteen in the Air Training Corps he took a gliding course in a two-seater training glider from Lossiemouth. 'Fearless and quick to learn' was the report from his instructor.

Next year he flew solo and qualified for his ATC gliding wings. Earlier he had notched up six 'O' levels in English Language and Literature, Mathematics, British History, French and General Science. In his final year at school he took three 'A' levels in History, English and Economics and Political Studies. Then he took a crash course at RAF Benson, Oxfordshire, flying solo in

The royal glider

An eighteenth birthday study of Prince Andrew at Buckingham Palace

a naval Chipmunk. Andrew had always wanted to be a flier and, with the example of his father and brother to spur him on, he decided on the navy as a career.

First of all, in 1978, he undertook parachute training with his elder brother. Slyly teasing him about his age, he said: 'You're getting on a bit for this sort of thing.' Charles was thirty at the time.

After the parachute training he did a three-day test to decide if he was the type for a naval career. He passed well and in September 1979, Andrew, by then a six-foot tall, broad-shouldered and physically tough specimen, entered the Britannia Naval College, Dartmouth.

In 1980 while on leave he began earning his reputation as a playboy. He toured the night clubs, even being re-

Practising a parachute jump; the Prince of Wales with Prince Andrew

Prince Andrew stands proudly in front of his helicopter

Mission accomplished: after a parachute jump

fused entry to Annabel's because because he was not wearing a tie. Eventually they loaned him one but he never forgot that rule again. At 'Trader Jon's', Florida, also in 1980, the stripper who had entertained Andrew and his shipmates from HMS *Hermes* renamed her act 'The Randy Andy Eye Popper'.

By 1981 he was reckoned 'one of the lads' and his CO at Culdrose, the naval air station in Cornwall, had to pin up a notice forbidding the Queen's son and his fellow officers from watching blue movies on the mess video.

He passed out of Culdrose a qualified helicopter pilot with top prize for his course. For the Duke of Edinburgh who had flown himself to Cornwall to present Andrew with his 'wings', it was a proud day.

A word from the Lord High Admiral, the Queen, as Prince Andrew passes out of

Dartmouth, 1980

A PRINCE
GROWS UP

COURAGEOUS IN BATTLE, PRINCE ANDREW WAS NOT
ASHAMED TO ADMIT HIS FEAR AND TALK OF THE
LONELINESS OF WAR. IT WAS A STATE OF MIND WHICH
LATER, BACK IN PEACETIME BRITAIN, DOMINATED
HIS NEW HOBBY. 'LONELINESS IS A THEME OF MY
PHOTOGRAPHY,' HE SAID.

IT MAY HAVE STEMMED FROM REACTION TO
THE END OF HIS LOVE AFFAIR WITH KOO STARK, A
FORMER GIRL FRIEND. OR THE REALIZATION THAT
LIFE IN A PALACE COULD BE FULL OF RESTRICTIONS
FOR A YOUNG MAN WHO HAS KNOWN THE EASY-GOING
WORLD — OFF DUTY — OF A HELICOPTER PILOT.

rince Andrew had celebrated his twenty-first
birthday in February 1981 in the wardroom
mess at Culdrose, Cornwall, just before the ceremony at which he was presented his 'wings' by his
father. But the Queen decided a bigger party was called
for and held a summer ball for him at Windsor Castle.
The ancient fortress was floodlit and dancing went on
until dawn.

Then, on 29 July 1981, Andrew stood as 'supporter'
to his brother Charles when he married Diana Spencer in
St Paul's Cathedral. He wore his midshipman's uniform
as he was still a 'snottie' – so called because the uniform
originally had three buttons on the jacket sleeves on
which generations of 'snotties' are said to have wiped
their noses! But Andrew's uniform carried rather special
decorations that day: he wore the CVO (Commander of
the Royal Victorian Order) and the Jubilee medal.

By October 1981, he was commissioned as a Sub-
Lieutenant and posted to 820 Squadron on HMS *Invincible*
to be trained in anti-submarine warfare in the North

A bearded Prince Andrew is greeted by his grandmother

Prince Andrew, standing right, with the Prince and Princess of Wales after their

Atlantic. The aircraft carrier had a crew of 930 with 107 officers, and the Prince was known as 'H' for Highness.

When General Galtieri's troops invaded the Falklands in April 1982, *Invincible* was, inevitably, in the front line. Andrew insisted on accompanying his ship, and threatened to resign his commission if the fact that he was then second in line to the throne prevented him from going. Prime Minister Margaret Thatcher consulted her cabinet and it was agreed – with the Queen's permission – that he should sail with the Task Force.

HMS *Invincible* was a premier target for the Argentine

Prince Andrew with America's First Lady, Nancy Reagan

Prince Philip (right) with a bearded Prince Andrew (centre) and Prince Edward. (Right) Prince Andrew writes all his own speeches. Here he is speaking in 1981

That familiar royal grin

air force, particularly with a British prince on board. At least three times Argentine radio reported her sunk but, thankfully, she came back to Portsmouth unscathed.

Andrew was co-pilot of a Sea King Mark V anti-submarine helicopter – one of thirty-three in the Task Force. It carried either four torpedoes or four depth charges and ferried men and supplies, engaged in search and rescue missions in freezing, often stormy weather, and protected the carrier by acting as a decoy for Exocet missiles.

When HMS *Sheffield* was hit Prince Andrew was airborne above *Invincible*. 'For the first ten minutes we really didn't know which way to turn and what to do,' he says. 'I knew where I was and I was fairly frightened.'

He was airborne again when he saw the *Atlantic Conveyor* destroyed. It was his worst experience, he said, helping to lift the wounded from the ship. 'The weather was dreadful,' says a survivor. 'It was very cold and the waves were about twenty feet high. We were like sardines in our raft, one on top of another.'

Prince Andrew and his co-pilot took their helicopter down to the tops of the waves, at considerable personal risk. Later it was described as one of the bravest acts of the campaign – but as Andrew pointed out, all the pilots were doing it.

He said afterwards: 'I saw it [*Atlantic Conveyor*] being struck by the missile and it was something I'll never forget. It was horrific.'

During the campaign A. J. McIlroy, the *Daily Telegraph* correspondent with the Task Force, wrote that life on *Invincible* was too hectic for protocol. 'Anyway he wouldn't have wanted it,' says a petty officer. 'He expects us to treat him like all the others and there is no side to him at all.'

The Prince's commanding officer, Commander Ralph Wykes-Sneyd, whose job it was to order him into battle, says: 'He was a very capable young man; an above-average pilot; professional and very sound. There were about fifty officers in the Squadron and he got on very well with them all. They were an extrovert bunch and he mixed in very well. You may have blue blood but the royal tag doesn't rate much mustard.'

The change in Andrew was obvious after the Falklands. He matured in the loneliness of battle in the South Atlantic. As he said himself: 'I guess I had to, after seeing what I had and feeling what I had felt.'

He spoke of the loneliness of war. 'That is the thing that stands out. It is never more lonely than when you are lying on deck with missiles flying around. You are on your own.'

After the campaign it was said that 'one of the most refreshing aspects of Prince Andrew's personality is the candour and honesty which make him unashamed to admit fear. A hero most of the time is an ordinary man who keeps perfectly natural fears under control, accepting risks as part of a sense of duty but well aware of their nature nevertheless.'

The Prince came home to a hero's welcome, as did every other Falklands veteran, and deeply committed to a naval career. Sir John Junor, never one to compliment a 'royal' lightly, was moved to write in the *Sunday Express*: 'He is a one-off. A fizzer. With clearly an enormous potential for leadership. We are out of our minds if we make him spend most of the rest of his life walking around, hands behind his back, opening church bazaars.'

Prince Andrew enlarged on his Falklands experience in a BBC interview: 'Everybody was frightened, I'm absolutely certain. I think that, to a large degree, if you're not frightened then you make a mistake.'

Back home the Queen missed her second son immensely but tried to be light-hearted outside the immediate family. A visitor had said: 'You must be missing Prince Andrew while he is serving overseas.'

The Queen replied: 'Yes, indeed I do, especially as he is the only one in the family who knows how to work the video.'

The visitor went on: 'I should have thought Prince Philip would have been able to do that.'

The Queen smiled: 'In that case you have clearly never flown with him.'

But the strain of having a son in active service began

HMS Invincible

The Prince's helicopter coming into land

to tell – as it did for every other mother with a son in the Task Force. The Queen had tired eyes and a tight-lipped, unsmiling mouth on public engagements as the weeks wore on, betraying her understandable tension.

It must have been a deeply happy moment when, soon after the Argentine surrender, the telephone in her sitting-room rang early one evening and Prince Andrew's cheerful voice was on the line. 'I made the call and she was in,' he said later. 'It was about the right time of the evening. She was quite surprised to hear my voice.'

When HMS *Invincible* with Sub-Lieutenant HRH

Helicopter pilot, HRH the Prince Andrew

Prince Andrew, a rose between his teeth, returns from the Falklands

Andrew was brimming over with high spirits when he set foot on land. He tore off his cap and leapt into the air. Then with a rose, presented by a young girl, clenched between his teeth, he greeted the families of his shipmates.

Before leaving for a holiday with his family at Balmoral he spoke of the things he had missed, 'the smell of grass, silence . . . milk. I haven't had any real milk for five and a half months'.

But although the South Atlantic had matured Prince

The Prince waves his cap

The Prince Andrew on board returned to Portsmouth, the Queen, the Duke of Edinburgh and Princess Anne were there to meet it. The royal barge joined *Invincible* outside the harbour in the early morning mist and Andrew's family climbed aboard. It was the first royal 'perk' he had received and together, with 1,000 service-men aboard, they sailed into Portsmouth to an emotional and ecstatic welcome.

The Queen, her eyes shining with tears, stood close to Andrew as the band jubilantly played 'Land of Hope and Glory' and – in a salute to 820 Squadron – 'Those Magnificent Men In Their Flying Machines'.

His Royal Highness lays a wreath on the Cenotaph in Whitehall on Remembrance Sunday. (Left) The Prince at Portsmouth on his return from the Falklands

Koo Stark

Princess Margaret's house on the island of Mustique

Prince Andrew photographed at his aunt's house on Mustique

Andrew, there was still some emotional growing-up to do. The girl he'd left behind, Kathleen Dee-Anne Stark, known to millions – after her relationship with Andrew – simply as Koo, re-entered his life. She was an American-born actress who, unfortunately for their romance, had once appeared nude in a film that some described as 'soft porn'. And when the BBC showed an extract from the film on the evening news, it was clear Koo was going to be given a hard time.

Andrew believed himself to be deeply in love with Koo and she with him. There is no doubt that it was a very serious relationship and the Queen even invited her to Balmoral while Andrew was in the Falklands.

First he took her on the famous holiday to Princess Margaret's villa on Mustique. It is said the Queen paid the economy-class fare and they travelled as Mr and Mrs Cambridge. Koo's mother went along as chaperone but this did not impress the tabloids whose headlines screamed of 'passion under a tropical moon'.

Prince Andrew had only wanted a spell of peace and quiet with his girl-friend but was forced to return home after only a week. He loked tired and unhappy and was in a state of mind that made his family furious.

His loyal younger brother Edward said: 'He came back from that holiday more drawn, more tired than he had from three months of war. I think to treat someone who's just come back from serving his country like that is absolutely despicable.'

The Queen again invited Koo to Balmoral in an effort to ease the situation. But the Duke of Edinburgh reportedly spoke most seriously to Andrew pointing out how impossible a liaison it would be.

By Christmas when the royal family were together at Windsor, the romance was over – but they were still friends finding solace in a mutual interest in photography.

Since then Koo, although said to be stricken by Andrew's engagement to Sarah, has been both loyal and discreet. Andrew has always deeply appreciated her silence about their affair. In this both he and Sarah have been fortunate to have inspired affection and consequent discretion in their former loves.

Koo did marry briefly Timothy Jeffries, heir to the Green Shield Stamp fortune. But he was only twenty-two and friends say she was still in love with Andrew, so the marriage did not work out.

Andrew himself tried to forget her by taking out one glamorous girl after another. He had some unfortunate experiences when they tried to 'cash-in' on his friendship. One in particular, a comely model, Vicki Hodge, whom he met when *Invincible* was in the West Indies, betrayed his trust. She sold kiss-and-tell revelations to the media which did not go down well with his parents. Nor did the assortment of actresses and models who trailed after their son wherever he went. In America

Katie Rabbett, friend and model for many of Andrew's photographs

when he attended the Americas Cup Ball at Newport, Rhode Island, he was surrounded by them. Even when he returned to his old school, Lakefield in Canada, for a nostalgic visit, some of his old girl-friends turned up to wish him well.

The Queen decided he should represent her on the island of St Helena in 1984, and again the girls mobbed him. He picked one out to go disco dancing with – a local girl Deborah Yon.

On 15 September 1984, Prince Harry of Wales was born, and Prince Andrew was a god-father at his christen-ing in St George's Chapel, Windsor Castle. He is a favourite uncle to both the Wales boys, as he is to Princess Anne's children, Peter, and Zara (he is also god-father to the latter).

But still, in that year, Andrew himself had some more growing up to do. On a visit to America to raise money for British Olympic and Gordonstoun charities, he turned a paint-spraying gun on the press.

Yet it may all have been a mistake. He did tell his side of the story in a BBC interview later, saying: 'It was a complete accident and very unfortunate. I think I

The paint-spraying incident: Prince Andrew, wearing a satisfied look, turns on photographers

probably learnt my lesson to point the paint in the right direction – the next time.' But it didn't stop him enjoying the spectacle of a paint-splattered press corps. It cost £15,000 to repair the damage, however, and the bill was sent to the Palace.

He returned to Britain rather subdued and one headline asked: 'Clown prince or royal hooligan?' His parents were not amused and Andrew faced a dressing-down from a grim-faced Prince Philip on his return.

Nevertheless, it had been a salutory lesson and the criticism he suffered has not been wasted. For his next overseas trip on behalf of the Queen was counted a great success.

In the summer of 1985 he completed an eight-day tour of three provinces of Canada. It was his first solo major overseas trip, and he flew 8,500 miles to New Brunswick, Nova Scotia and Ontario, during leave from his new posting on board the frigate HMS *Brazen*.

All his old love for Canada resurfaced. 'When one starts in the family business one has to begin somewhere, and I can think of nowhere better to start than Canada,' says the Prince.

As usual, while in that country, he organized a weekend visit to his old school, Lakefield, of which he is extremely fond.

The trip in which he made twelve speeches, all written by himself, was praised by his hosts. 'Prince Andrew is a great ambassador for Britain and an asset to the royal family. He should be used more. He has got great charisma,' said Gerald Merrithew, Canada's Minister of State for Forestry.

'Prince Andrew's visit reinforced ties to the British crown and spread generous doses of good cheer,' said a Canadian newspaper.

The Prince himself spoke from the heart on behalf of youth, identifying himself with all young Canadians. 'We, the young people of our country, want also to con-

A thoroughly modern Prince in America

tribute to the development of our society. If we sometimes appear impatient it may be because we feel that the rest of you don't want our help and can jog along quite happily in the old way, thank you very much.'

'Bear with us please – we have much to give, if you will only let us,' he said.

Back on duty, Prince Andrew returned to the Falklands aboard HMS *Brazen* and caused a major panic by having to ditch his Lynx helicopter in a field when it developed a hydraulic fault.

A shower of hands greet Prince Andrew in a spontaneous welcome

Prince Andrew about to sign a visitors' book during a visit to Canada

The Prince of Wales and Prince Andrew in Canada

Poised for action

Said the Defence Ministry: '*Brazen*'s Lynx helicopter flown by Lieutenant Prince Andrew made a safe but unscheduled landing in a field in East Falkland.' The Queen, who hates flying in helicopters and is always nervous of them, was told of the incident.

Back in Britain Prince Andrew met Sarah Ferguson again and started taking her out when he managed to get leave in London. He also made several new friends in the photographic world – most notably Gene Nocon,

an American photographer who is one of the best in the business when it comes to the techniques of printing.

His interest in photography became an important part of his life away from the navy. It led to the publication of a book of his pictures of which he is really proud. Says a friend: 'He has the temperament of an artist and desperately wants his photography to be taken seriously.'

Andrew has learnt a lot in a few short years – perhaps the most important lesson, as far as his hobby is concerned, is that he will have to develop much more flair with his photographs before he can join the 'masters'.

The Prince at Sandringham, a Purdy tucked under his arm

Andrew and 'Fergie' at Windsor

Avening Court, Gloucestershire, mooted as a possible residence for the royal couple

The Prince has a dark room in Buckingham Palace and he improvises one in his navy quarters wherever he is. He is determined to go on learning and it may be that if he maintains his interest, photography could become his second career when he leaves the navy, probably in 1992.

'Loneliness is a theme of my photography,' he told David Frost in an interview. 'I am a recluse.'

Now he is married to Sarah that remark is decidedly out of date.

So is he a 'Hooray Henry', a sexy glamour boy who has well earned his nickname 'Randy Andy' and the description, attributed to Prince Charles, of 'the one with the Robert Redford looks'? Or is he 'H' for Highness as his Royal Navy colleagues, showing rather more than usual respect for a shipmate, know him? Outgoing, often arrogant but always fearless? An apparent extrovert who has, nevertheless, known spells of deep isolation and described himself as 'lonely' and 'a recluse'?

Whichever description is correct it is certain that Prince Andrew is an interesting mix of contradictions. He does have a charisma that owes more to the Mountbatten-Bowes Lyon side of his ancestry than to the more

His Royal Highness The Prince Andrew, an engagement study taken at Buckingham Palace

phlegmatic Windsors. He is a more complicated character than is first appreciated, with a strong personality tempered under battle conditions such as his father, the Duke of Edinburgh, knew in the Second World War at the Battle of Matapan and his grandfather, King George VI, experienced during the Battle of Jutland in the First World War.

'Before the Falklands it was easy to categorize him – he was very "I am Prince Andrew", rather noisy and full of childish "Hooray Henry" japes,' says a friend who has known Andrew since schooldays.

'But when he came back he was more thoughtful and introspective.' He was still chasing beautiful actresses and models, but when the romance with Koo Stark ended some time before the fateful meeting with Sarah Ferguson at Royal Ascot, Prince Andrew said to another friend: 'I am a loner – I really am. Yet when I say that no one believes me. I'd really like to be married but I've yet to meet the right girl.'

Now he has Sarah by his side; the bachelor days of

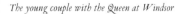
The young couple with the Queen at Windsor

Prince Andrew at the launch of his first book. (Right) Photographer at work

girl-chasing are behind him. So too, hopefully, are those feelings of loneliness and isolation known to have often been experienced at some time in their lives by others in his family.

Prince Andrew is succeeding in establishing his own identity and coming to terms with the private frustrations of being a royal prince. In this he will be able to help his wife, as she encounters some of the problems and pressures that the Princess of Wales, for example, has experienced. In turn, Sarah will encourage Andrew to work on the rudiments he already has of that ingredient princes must possess if they are to be popular – the common touch.

SARAH
AND DIANA

THE FRIENDSHIP OF DIANA AND SARAH, THE ROYAL
FAMILY'S MOST DECORATIVE PERSONALITIES IN THE
GLOWING FAMILY TAPESTRY, COULD BE A MOST
IMPORTANT FACTOR IN THE FUTURE OF THE
MOUNTBATTEN–WINDSOR DYNASTY.

EVERY FAMILY LEANS ON ITS OTHER MEMBERS FOR
SYMPATHETIC SUPPORT; THE ROYAL FAMILY, PRIVATELY
ISOLATED WITHIN ITS OWN CIRCLE, DO MORE THAN MOST.

THE PRINCESSES, WHO WILL SET THE STYLE FOR
FUTURE GENERATIONS, ARE EXTREMELY GOOD
FRIENDS. THEIR CLOSENESS IS EVIDENT IN THE MANY
APPEARANCES AT PRIVATE FUNCTIONS, PARTICULARLY
ON THE POLO FIELD WHERE THEY GOSSIP AND LAUGH
TOGETHER.

'The Princess of Wales and I are extremely good friends and we naturally talk about a lot of different subjects,' said Sarah in reply to a question about her close friendship with Diana.

To those who knew them well that carefully worded answer affirmed the bond between the two women, now sisters-in-law, which has been a most significant factor in this latest royal wedding. It promises to be a sustaining influence which may well enhance the contribution they both make to the monarchy of the future.

In the years ahead it will be Diana as Queen and Sarah as senior royal Duchess who will be the matriarchal, if not monarchial, royal figure-heads. They will take the womanly place, in the natural progression of time, of the Queen and the Queen Mother, the two senior royal ladies at present.

That scenario seems far away as the twentieth century ebbs and the royal family prepare for a changing world in the twenty-first century.

But the secure future of the monarchy is never far from the Queen's mind and her advisers are conscious that the close friendship between Diana and Sarah has been a source of pleasure to their mother-in-law. It augurs well for the continuation of the closely knit family life that has supported the royal family for the past fifty years, largely due to the example of the Queen's parents, King George VI and his wife, now Queen Elizabeth, the Queen Mother.

'Palace pals' and 'the royal twin-set' are two light-hearted descriptions by the media of the alter-ego relationship between Diana and Sarah that has been accentuated by their new kinship.

Complete contrasts in appearance and character, they are still cast in a similar mould. Tall with good looks that are typically British; Diana – just over eighteen months younger than Sarah – is the blonde Anglo-Saxon,

maturing into a cool, classical beauty. Always faultlessly dressed, she is at her sympathetic best with children, the old or sick. Sarah is the fiery-haired Celt with an outward aura that is perhaps more *simpatico*; warm and vital, she is one of life's givers.

A member of the Fleet Street 'rat-pack' has cause to remember her kindness. He had been sent down to Sarah's home where she was spending the week-end prior to the engagement announcement.

She opened the door and said: 'I'm not going out – but they'll expect you to get a picture. I mustn't pose – but will this do?' Framed in the doorway she made an excellent shot. The photographer bothered the Ferguson family no more that weekend and everyone was happy.

It is true that Sarah is older and more experienced than Diana was when she became a member of the royal family. But now nobody knows better than the Princess of Wales how difficult a transition it is when a newcomer joins 'the firm'. Princess Michael of Kent, no stranger to the difficulties that can arise, once said that nothing prepares you for that experience.

Initially, Diana found life in the over-protected atmosphere of a royal home could be isolated – 'like being behind a glass curtain' was how Marion Crawford, governess to the Queen and Princess Margaret as children, described it.

No matter how close and loving her marriage is, a Princess, imprisoned to a certain extent by her position, can find life both lonely and frustrating. It is true that being a member of the royal family has its compensations. It is, above all, a rewarding and fulfilling job when it is done well.

As Sarah has seen from her friendship with Diana, a British princess – even in these days – is a privileged creature. As Prince Andrew's wife she will never again have to worry about being late for trains and planes or having enough cash to pay the electricity bill. But, like

Diana, she will miss the everyday freedoms, which until now she will have taken for granted.

Although the Duke of Edinburgh has talked of how his children go shopping and enjoy pubs just like everyone else, there is not much fun when there is constant security vigilance.

Sarah's assumption that she would be able to continue her job as a publisher was a brave attempt at normality. But already the difficulty has arisen that she cannot work for a commercial enterprise under a royal roof.

Nor is it easy just simply to go to the office each morning. Three security men would be the minimum needed to guard the Queen's daughter-in-law in an age when her family are top terrorist targets.

'Perhaps she can continue on a consultancy basis,' suggested the Duke of Edinburgh. But as his other daughter-in-law Diana knows it is difficult to live a normal life as a Princess.

Diana, of course, never attempted to keep on her job because, as the wife of the Prince of Wales and future

Sarah Ferguson with Diana, Princess of Wales

Great friends. Sarah with the Princess of Wales at Smith's Lawn, Windsor Great Park

Sarah and Diana together at polo

Queen, she already has one – with an increasingly heavy load of public engagements.

For Sarah, being a working wife would help ease the loneliness when her husband is away on naval duties. As Prince Andrew said: 'I think she will be a remarkable wife . . . and I know how difficult it is, talking to other naval colleagues of mine about what it is like being married to a naval officer, because we do spend so much time away.'

This factor makes the friendship Sarah has with her sister-in-law even more important. Prince Philip once said that 'the children' soon find out the only people they can really talk to is one of the family.

Now the two Princesses each have someone who is not only a relative by marriage, but a real friend. They have so much in common besides the marriage of 'Sloane and throne', as the *Daily Mail* put it.

Both come from within the charmed circle; bred from old families descended (on the wrong side of the blanket) from the Stuart monarchs.

The Princess of Wales has six direct descents from King Charles I, five of them through Charles II's illegitimate children. Sarah has six descents from Charles II and is a fourth cousin to Diana through their ancestress Louise de Kéroualle, the Frenchwoman who became Charles II's mistress and whom he later created Duchess of Portsmouth. More recently the common denominator in their shared ancestry was James Hamilton, 1st Duke of Abercorn, great-great-great-grandfather of them both.

In present generations, Diana's brother-in-law, Robert Fellowes – the Queen's deputy private secretary, who is married to her elder sister Jane – is a first cousin of Sarah's father Major Ronald Ferguson.

Although they are distantly related, it was not blood links but polo that, initially, drew Diana and Sarah together. During the spring and early summer of 1981, after her engagement had become official, Diana found herself in a whole new world when she went to watch Prince Charles play at Smith's Lawn, Windsor. It was a game everybody seemed to assume she understood. Yet it was Sarah – who really had grown up with the sport – who explained the finer points of the game to a mystified Diana. When the younger girl clearly became bored, they retreated behind the pony lines to relax and gossip.

There are so many photographs of the two young women together to illustrate the early days of their friendship. As photographers snapped away at Diana they constantly moaned about the other girl who was always in the picture. One of them, Jayne Fincher, remembers saying, 'There's that redhead again – wish she'd move over and get out of Di's way.' She now regrets she didn't take more pictures of Andrew's future wife.

After her marriage, Diana who found she was often under pressure in her new role, discovered she could unburden herself to Sarah, who became a regular at the intimate Kensington Palace lunches the Princess of Wales likes to give for a few close girl-friends. In turn, Diana heard all about Sarah's love affair with Paddy McNally and, when the relationship began to founder, she helped console her friend. Was there, even then, a match-making gleam in Diana's eye?

Although the friendship between the two girls was to come later, their early lives followed curiously similar patterns. Both, in their childhood, grew up in the shadow of the royal family – Diana at Park House, Sandringham, and Sarah at Lowood, near Windsor Castle. Diana was playing with Prince Andrew at Sandringham about the same time as he first met Sarah at Windsor.

'Fergie' greets the Prince and Princess of Wales

Early days. Sarah Ferguson and the Princess of Wales at Smith's Lawn, Windsor, 1982

Royal greeting: the Princess of Wales and Sarah at a polo match

Sharing a joke

Into both their lives also came the personal tragedy of broken marriages between their parents. Their mothers, whom they adored, left home to live with someone else. The girls stayed behind, in the care of their fathers. Diana was only six and Sarah thirteen when this happened.

Diana's mother, Frances, left four children to run away with and later marry wall-paper heir Peter Shand-Kydd. Sarah's mother, Susan, left her home and three children because she was in love with Argentinian polo player Hector Barrantes whom she eventually married.

Both girls' fathers were understandably greatly upset. Suddenly, they had to fill a dual role; but they coped well with the problems involved. Nevertheless, both Diana and Sarah had some difficult childhood years which has made them determined to cherish their own family lives.

'There is no substitute for a mother,' comments Major Ferguson. 'It was hard alone,' says Lord Spencer.

In both families a much-loved grandmother became the corner-stone which helped hold them all together. Both Princesses acknowledge the debt they owe to these two women who were, in fact, second cousins – the late Countess Spencer and Lady Elmhirst, Sarah's grandmother. Diana also had the loving guidance of her maternal grandmother, Lady Fermoy, who like her father's mother the late Countess Spencer, is an old friend and lady-in-waiting of the Queen Mother.

Wisely, the grandmothers encouraged Diana and Sarah to divide their love between both parents and they have always remained close to their mothers, whilst living with their fathers.

Diana's mother, Mrs Shand-Kydd, lives on the island of Seil in Argyllshire in north-west Scotland where her husband runs a sheep farm. At one time she owned and served in a newsagent shop and then a toy shop in Oban. Diana and her sisters were frequent visitors and their mother has been an important influence in their lives.

'Sarah and I are very close,' says Mrs Hector Barrantes who lives quietly with her husband in Argentina, 400 miles from the bright lights of the capital city, Buenos Aires. They have a 1,000-acre farm where they grow wheat, maize and sunflowers and breed between 600 and 800 polo ponies.

'Susie' Barrantes, as she likes to be called, loves dogs and has eight of them – a Jack Russell terrier, a labrador, three Irish wolf hounds and three Basset hounds. Like Frances Shand-Kydd and her husband, Susie and Hector Barrantes are very happy together and Susie is delighted that, despite the distance separating them, her relationship with Sarah and her sister Jane is as close as ever.

Mrs Barrantes had met the Queen many times when she was married to Sarah's father. They were regularly invited to Windsor and Sandringham but her husband had only met members of the royal family informally on the polo ground – before the war with Argentina. Some weeks before Sarah's wedding the Queen invited her mother and step-father to tea during Ascot races. There Hector Barrantes was formally presented to the Queen in the presence of the Prince and Princess of Wales. Prince Andrew and Sarah, who were also there, helped over tea and chocolate cake to ease a meeting that could have been awkward.

Destined to live in royal palaces, Diana and Sarah were brought up in family homes – one considerably grander than the other.

The Spencers of Althorp, the family seat in Northamptonshire, lived in a 450-year-old stately home, set in 1,500 acres. Sarah's smaller but beautiful home, Dummer Down House, was inherited from Major Ferguson's father. Its 800-acre estate nestles at the foot of the south western slopes of Farleigh Hill near Basingstoke.

Both Sarah and Diana experienced the trauma familiar to children of divorced parents who marry again. Both know the 'wicked step-mother' syndrome, though for Sarah it was always a joke. She loved her stepmother from the start and made life easy for her when she joined the family.

Lost in a sea of faces, Charles, Diana and Sarah

A kiss for the Prince of Wales at Smith's Lawn, Windsor Great Park. (Right) Prince Andrew with his sister-in-law at a country wedding in 1985

The Queen with Sarah's mother at Smith's Lawn

Sarah with her mother

In Diana's case the relationship was not at first easy when her father married Raine, the former Countess of Dartmouth and daughter of romantic novelist Barbara Cartland. However, following Lord Spencer's serious illness (he suffered a stroke in the late 1970s), during which his wife's devoted care helped restore him to health, his family have appreciated their stepmother more.

A love of children is another thing Sarah and Diana have in common. Both want several of their own: 'It would be quite fun to have quite a few,' says Sarah. Diana, of course, not only has two of her own already but was a popular nursery-school teacher before her marriage. Sarah has her three young half-brother and sisters who have provided her with plenty of baby-sitting experience.

In the late spring of 1985, the Queen, in her kindly way, asked the Princess of Wales if there was anyone she would like to invite to the Ascot house party at Windsor Castle in June. 'Andrew will have leave then –

Ronald Ferguson, the Princess of Wales and Prince William

do you know an attractive girl to partner him?' the Queen is said to have asked.

Diana suggested her friend Sarah Ferguson, whom the Queen, of course, had known since she was a child. The coveted invitation in the large square envelope with the royal cipher was duly sent. It was to herald so many changes in Sarah's life – although when she first saw it her immediate reaction, say friends, was to worry about what clothes she'd need for such a 'dressy' occasion as Royal Ascot week.

Here the Princess of Wales was able to help with advice and, as the world knows, the romance of Sarah and Andrew began at the race-meeting.

As their love deepened it became obvious to Diana who knew them both so well, that Cupid could do with some right royal help. She enlisted Prince Charles's

With the Queen at the Royal Windsor Horse Show

Sarah and Diana have always exchanged confidences

At Smith's Lawn after a day at Ascot, 1986

support which was not difficult because he liked Sarah immensely and, as he said when asked to comment on their engagement, 'I'm prejudiced.'

They invited Sarah to join their party for their ski-ing holiday at Klosters, Switzerland – the most public acknowledgement of their support so far. Earlier, too,

The Princess of Wales, Sarah Ferguson and Prince William visit Prince Andrew on board HMS Brazen

there was the visit to Prince Andrew's ship, HMS *Brazen* when Sarah, wearing an outfit borrowed from Diana, accompanied her and Prince William for a tour of the ship.

After Prince Andrew's proposal, the Prince and Princess of Wales were the first members of the royal family to hear, in great secrecy, their happy news.

Diana was delighted that she and Sarah were to be sisters-in-law. But she knew only too well how many pitfalls there were in learning the job of being a royal princess, not always obvious to an ordinary girl.

'There is no better way of learning than by the

Leaving Ascot for Smith's Lawn, June 1986

Prince Andrew and Sarah join members of the royal family on the Palace balcony after the Trooping of the Colour, June 1986

example of the others,' said a courtier. Now Diana set out to help her friend adjust to her changed life style.

In this she was supported by everyone in the royal family from the Queen downwards. 'We must make her feel welcome and at home,' said Her Majesty.

But it was Diana, who knew the world Sarah was exchanging for marriage and a place in history, who understood best. She, too, had earned a living, shopped in chain stores and hopped on the tube. She could appreciate how anxious Sarah was to become familiar with the protocol of a royal court and the life she would be expected to live as Prince Andrew's wife.

Diana has perfected the polished look of one of the world's best-dressed women. Now she tactfully tried to guide Sarah's choice of clothes.

But Andrew's girl is a very individual character and does not want to be a carbon-copy of the Princess of Wales, however close they are. Nor, it must be remembered, does she have unlimited cash for couture clothes.

Sometimes her choice of outfit does not conform with the views of fashion editors who have been both frank and cruel in their appraisal of her fashion sense. 'Of course it hurts when they write unkindly,' says a Ferguson family friend. To most people, however, including without doubt her husband, it is more important to have a lively, attractive woman of character than a fashionable clothes horse.

It is simply not Sarah's style and, as her father advised her before she left for the Queen's house-party at Windsor, the really important thing is to 'just be yourself'.

In the early days she did borrow clothes occasionally from Diana, but she is rapidly evolving her own look to match her very distinctive hair and personality.

As another red-head, actress Jane Asher, wrote in the *Daily Mail*: 'Red-heads it seems may be about to enjoy a renaissance. Yes, it's about time we had a royal patron; its been a long wait since Elizabeth I and some of us feel she tended to over-indulge in our well-known activity of losing her temper.'

Sarah's glorious hair is already being tamed to lie under the tiaras and hats that are, on formal occasions, obligatory for the women members of the royal family. Says Denise of Michael-John who does her hair: 'She has lovely red, naturally curly hair in very good condition. What style she chooses will depend on what she is going to wear, the shape of the neckline – she can wear her hair in so many ways.'

Somewhere in the Queen's fabulous collection of jewellery are pieces Sarah will inherit. Diana already has some beautiful jewels presented by her mother-in-law. The latest, a large sapphire brooch she wore on a visit to Vienna, was so enormous it was difficult to pin on to material. So, on the advice of Princess Michael, it became the centre-piece for a six-strand pearl necklace.

It was an admirable example of how one princess can help another, as Sarah and Diana have already discovered.

With the advent of the newcomer to their ranks, the contrasting personalities of all the royal princesses of the younger generation – the Princess of Wales, Princess Anne, the two royal Duchesses of Gloucester and Kent and Princess Michael of Kent, are beginning to knit together into a style that should strengthen the Queen's family through whatever lies ahead.

A wistful study of the royal bride-to-be

WEDDINGS IN THE ABBEY

'A PRINCELY MARRIAGE,' WROTE WALTER BAGEHOT, THE VICTORIAN CONSTITUTIONAL EXPERT, 'IS THE BRILLIANT EDITION OF A UNIVERSAL FACT AND AS SUCH IT RIVETS MANKIND.'

WHATEVER ONE'S VIEWS OF THE MONARCHY AND ITS FUNCTION, FEW CAN DENY THAT IT ADDS CHARM, DIGNITY, GRACEFULNESS AND COLOUR TO A WORLD WHICH IS BECOMING INCREASINGLY BEREFT OF SUCH QUALITIES. THE MONARCHY ALSO ADDS AN ELEMENT OF FANTASY TO THE BRITISH WAY OF LIFE, AND NEVER IS THIS SEEN TO BETTER ADVANTAGE THAN WHEN A FULL-SCALE ROYAL PAGEANT IS MOUNTED.

(Left) The marriage of Princess Alexandra and the Hon. Angus Ogilvy, Westminster Abbey, 1963

Long before it became associated with royal weddings, Westminster Abbey had established itself in the public consciousness as the place where England's kings and queens are traditionally crowned. Properly known as the Collegiate Church of St Peter in Westminster, the present Abbey was founded by King Henry III (1216–72), on the site of an eleventh-century church built by Edward the Confessor, whose tomb lies immediately behind the High Altar in the thirteenth-century chapel dedicated to his name. It is in this chapel that royal marriage registers are signed and here, too, that after the great Coronation ceremonies, kings and queens are arrayed in their robes of state.

That Westminster Abbey became a setting for royal weddings less than seventy years ago, was due entirely to the personal modesty of one princess. She was Patricia of Connaught, the younger daughter of Prince Arthur, Duke of Connaught, and a granddaughter of Queen Victoria. 'Princess Pat', as she was popularly known, asked that her wedding to Commander the Honourable Alexander Ramsay, Royal Navy, on 27 February 1919, should be solemnized in a church more in keeping with her status as a junior member of the royal family. She chose Westminster Abbey.

Hitherto most royal weddings had been celebrated in one of two places. The first was the Chapel Royal,

Princess Patricia of Connaught and her bridegroom, February 1919

The wedding of the Princess Mary and Viscount Lascelles, 1922. Standing second from left, Lady Elizabeth Bowes Lyon, now the Queen Mother

St James's Palace, where, on 10 February 1840, the 21-year-old Queen Victoria married her cousin, Prince Albert of Saxe-Coburg-Gotha, and where, fifty-three years later, on 6 July 1893, the future King George V and Queen Mary – then Prince George, Duke of York and Princess Victoria Mary of Teck – knelt before the altar on their wedding-day.

The second location was St George's Chapel, Windsor Castle. Here four of Queen Victoria's nine children – including the future Edward VII – and many of her grandchildren, among them Princess Alice, Countess of Athlone, were married. In choosing Westminster Abbey, therefore, Princess Patricia of Connaught – who upon her marriage relinquished her royal titles to become plain Lady Patricia Ramsay – unwittingly set a precedent that eight members of the royal family have now followed.

The first, in 1922, was George V's only daughter Mary, who later became the Princess Royal. Her marriage to Henry, Viscount Lascelles, later sixth Earl of Harewood, took place on 28 February, the day after Lady

Prince Albert, Duke of York, marries Lady Elizabeth Bowes Lyon, 26 April 1923

Patricia's first wedding anniversary. But unlike the Ramsays' wedding, which was more 'high-society' in tone, that of the Princess Mary, with all its attendant pageantry, could not have been mistaken for anything but a royal event. Among the Princess's bridesmaids that day was one young woman who, only fourteen months later, became a royal bride herself. She was Prince Andrew's grandmother, then, of course, the Lady Elizabeth Bowes Lyon.

The youngest child of the seventeenth Earl of Strathmore and Kinghorne, Lady Elizabeth had twice refused proposals of marriage from Prince Albert, Duke of York, the second son of George V and Queen Mary. Indeed, it was only when 'Bertie', as the future George VI was known to his family, plucked up enough courage to propose for the third time, that Lady Elizabeth finally accepted him. Three months later, on 26 April 1923, Elizabeth Bowes Lyon became Her Royal Highness the Duchess of York.

'She drove to the Abbey in the simplest possible manner,' chirped one newspaper columnist of the day. 'On her return all was changed. From a commoner she became as if by magic the fourth lady in the land. . . .' Yet no matter how popular the Duke of York and his bride were with the nation, none was more adored than Bertie's elder brother, the dashing young Prince of Wales. In every respect he represented 'golden youth' the whole world over, and it was, of course, to his eventual marriage that the nation and empire looked forward with the keenest anticipation. What could not have been foretold in April 1926 was that this prince, still a bachelor when he succeeded his father as King Edward VIII in January 1936, would be forced to abdicate in order to marry the woman with whom he fell so hopelessly in love.

Two years before the Abdication crisis, however, the nation was to welcome the marriage of the Prince of

Prince Andrew's grandparents, 1923; the future King George VI and Queen Elizabeth on their wedding day

Wales's favourite brother, Prince George, Duke of Kent. With the sole exception of the present Duke of Edinburgh, Prince George's bride, the beautiful Princess Marina of Greece and Denmark, was the last member of a foreign royal family to marry into the Royal House of Windsor. Thereafter, princes and princesses, as with the Duke of York and Princess Mary, had very little choice but to look for partners among the higher echelons of British society or, at all events, from among sufficiently acceptable families of comfortable, upper-class backgrounds. Thus the wedding of Prince George and Princess Marina, on 29 November 1934, witnessed not only a *royal* wedding in the truest tradition, but Britain's final alliance with another royal house.

Unstable at the best of times, the Greek monarchy was deposed and restored with almost comic regularity. In 1934, Princess Marina and her parents – Prince Nicholas of Greece and his wife Helen, born a Russian Grand Duchess – were living in Paris, in what was the eleventh year of the Greek royal family's latest exile. Tall, sophisticated and as elegant as it was possible for a far from rich refugee to be, Princess Marina worked as a mannequin for some of the greatest Parisian couturiers, including the House of Molyneux, who were to make her elegant shimmering white and silver wedding dress.

Princess Marina's engagement to Prince George, Duke of Kent, was an event which delighted the British and won a popularity for the Princess herself, that lasted until her death in 1968 at the age of only sixty-one. Indeed, during her wedding service, the Archbishop of Canterbury, Dr Lang, reminded her of the trust she now held 'in ministering to the needs of the good British folk, who have already, with a warmth so swift and spontaneous, taken you into their hearts'. Of the new Duchess of Kent's eight bridesmaids at Westminster Abbey on that wintry day more than half a century ago,

The wedding of Prince George, Duke of Kent and Princess Marina of Greece and Denmark. Sitting at left, the present Queen, then Princess Elizabeth, November 1934

Princess Elizabeth and Philip, Duke of Edinburgh before the High Altar at Westminster Abbey

no fewer than six were royal princesses. They were the Grand Duchess Kira of Russia, Princess Juliana (later Queen) of the Netherlands, and the Greek princesses Irene, Eugenie and Katherine. But quite the youngest of the royal attendants was the eight-year-old Princess Elizabeth of York, niece of the bridegroom and, of course, Britain's future queen, Elizabeth II.

Thirteen years later in November 1947, Princess Elizabeth – by now aged twenty-one, and Heiress Presumptive to the throne of her father, King George VI – became the fifth royal bride to be married at Westminster Abbey.

She was to marry Philip, Duke of Edinburgh (as he was created on the eve of his wedding). Like his cousin, Princess Marina, Philip had been born a member of the Greek royal family. The only son of Prince Andrew of Greece and Princess Alice of Battenberg, he had been

educated in Britain and, like his maternal uncle 'Dickie', Earl Mountbatten of Burma, served the Royal Navy with distinction. In fact, it was at the Royal Navy College, Dartmouth, in July 1939, that the first recorded meeting between Prince Philip and Princess Elizabeth occurred. Philip had been detailed to look after his distant cousin while her parents inspected the college. In spite of his displeasure at having to amuse a slip of a girl barely into her teens, 'Lilibet', as she is privately known to her family, is said to have been entranced by the tall, blond prince.

A few years later, however, in true fairy-story tradition, the Prince and Princess had fallen in love and, on 10 July 1947, following the royal family's return from a tour of South Africa, their engagement was formally announced by the King and Queen.

Officially designated an 'austerity wedding' – the

Princess Elizabeth and Philip, Duke of Edinburgh, 20 November 1947

The royal bride and bridegroom

The balcony appearance at Buckingham Palace

Second World War had ended only two years before – London was still treated to a glittering pageant, the like of which had not been seen since a full decade earlier at the Coronation of George VI and Queen Elizabeth. Riding in the elaborate maroon and gold Irish State Coach, the King accompanied the bride, dressed in pearl-embroidered ivory duchess satin, to Westminster Abbey, with a full Sovereign's Escort of the Household Cavalry – 126 Troopers strong, all clad in ceremonial uniforms – in attendance.

At the Abbey a fanfare heralded Princess Elizabeth's arrival and, as the choir sang the processional hymn 'Praise my soul, the King of Heaven', the bride and her father, followed by two kilted page-boys, the Princes William of Gloucester and Michael of Kent, and eight bridesmaids, among them Princess Margaret and Princess Alexandra of Kent, slowly crossed the Nave to the steps

of the Sacrarium. There the future Queen and the newly created Duke of Edinburgh were married by the Archbishop of Canterbury, Dr Geoffrey Fisher. The essential simplicity of the service was stressed by the Archbishop in his address, when he told the congregation of 2,000, including more than twenty-five foreign royal guests, that 'notwithstanding the splendour and national significance of the service . . . it is the same as it would be for any cottager who might be married this afternoon in some small country church'.

Princess Elizabeth's wedding was an occasion which the nation was able to share on the day itself through the medium of radio, or the 'wireless', as it was then called, followed a little later by newsreel footage shown in the country's cinemas as a special presentation. By 1960 great advances in the science of broadcasting meant that the wedding of Princess Margaret and society photographer Antony Armstrong-Jones, on Friday 6 May, could be watched on televison. Of course, twenty-six years ago colour television was unknown in Britain, but while an estimated half a million people jammed themselves along the processional route to cheer Princess Margaret on her way to and from the Abbey, tens of thousands sat in front of their small screens at home, mesmerized by the 'live' transmission from Westminster.

Television coverage of the event wasn't the only innovation which made the wedding of the Queen's sister so memorable, however. For apart from the fact that this royal wedding – for all its glamour and pageantry – was a more 'intimate' affair than that of the then Princess Elizabeth, the bridegroom's background indicated a very significant change in royal attitudes. Not very long before, the chances of a man who made a living as a photographer marrying into the sovereign's immediate family were remote, to say the least. But after the unhappy outcome of Princess Margaret's romance with

the divorced Group-Captain Peter Townsend in October 1955, both the Queen and Queen Elizabeth the Queen Mother, were genuinely delighted at the Princess's happiness and it was, in the words of the official announcement, 'with the greatest pleasure' that the Queen gave her consent to Princess Margaret's marriage to the son of Ronald Armstrong-Jones Q.C., and his first wife Anne, Countess of Rosse.

Three years later, following in the footsteps of her parents – the Duke and Duchess of Kent – it was the turn of Princess Alexandra to be married before the High Altar at Westminster Abbey. She was the seventh member of the royal family to be married there. At the age of twenty-six 'Alex', as much of Fleet Street referred to the Princess, had established herself as one of the most popular, if most private, of royal personalities.

As a teenager she had been described by the American chronicler Chips Channon as 'a whirlwind of a girl', and so she was. Tall and rather awkward – her striding

A serene study of Princess Margaret after her wedding

Princess Margaret driving to her wedding

Princess Margaret and her bridegroom leave Westminster Abbey after their wedding, 6 May 1960

On the arm of her brother, Princess Alexandra makes her way along the Nave, 24 April 1963

Princess Alexandra, a classically beautiful bride

The Princess and her husband leaving the Abbey

walk was once likened to that of a 'farmer's wife' – Princess Alexandra represented the informal face of British royalty. For it was in her constant good humour and unfailing consideration of others that much of her appeal was to be found.

Unlike Tony Armstrong-Jones, who in October 1961 had been created the first Earl of Snowdon, Princess Alexandra's fiancée, the Honourable Angus Ogilvy, was born and raised within court circles. For over fifty years his grandmother, Mabell, Countess of Airlie, had been a lady-in-waiting to and a very close friend of Princess Alexandra's grandmother, Queen Mary. His father had been Lord Chamberlain to Queen Elizabeth the Queen

Mother from the time of her coronation in 1937 while, today, his brother, the Earl of Airlie, holds office as Lord Chamberlain, in succession to Lord Maclean; and his sister-in-law, the American-born Countess of Airlie, is an active member of the Royal Household in her role as an extra lady-in-waiting to the Queen.

Princess Alexandra and Angus Ogilvy had known each other for several years before even the slightest hint of romance was detected. In fact the Princess's name had been linked for some time with that of Lord O'Neill, while gossip columnists chattered about a possible marriage with Crown Prince Harald of Norway – a marriage, it must be said, that Princess Marina, ever

Princess Alexandra and the Hon. Angus Ogilvy at St James's Palace, after their wedding

mindful of rank and position, would certainly have welcomed. Instead Princess Alexandra fell in love with Angus Ogilvy and their engagement was finally announced on 29 November 1962. But for her father's tragic death twenty years earlier, that day would have been Prince George and Princess Marina's twenty-eighth wedding anniversary.

Five months later, on Wednesday 24 April 1963, Princess Alexandra, dressed entirely in magnolia lace, with her veil – twenty-one feet long – secured by the diamond tiara her mother had worn at her own wedding, left her home at Kensington Palace to drive to West-

minster Abbey. Given away by her elder brother Edward, the Duke of Kent, who two years earlier had married Miss Katharine Worsley at York Minster, the royal bride of 1963 was attended by two pageboys and five bridesmaids. Of the latter, two in particular were especially noteworthy: Princess Anne who, at thirteen, was chief bridesmaid and had suddenly started to look rather grown up, and the blonde, blue-eyed and mischievous Archduchess Elizabeth of Austria who, at the age of six, seemed determined to win more than her share of attention; notably by larking around with one of the pageboys, the Master of Ogilvy, while they were stand-

Princess Anne and Captain Mark Phillips at Buckingham Palace after their wedding on 14 November 1973

Princess Anne and Mark Phillips await the arrival of the Glass Coach after their wedding

ing under the Abbey awning, waiting for the Princess to arrive.

At the close of the ceremony, as the bride and bridegroom emerged from the Chapel of St Edward the Confessor, Princess Alexandra turned to her chief bridesmaid, saying, 'Your turn next.' With an expression of complete surprise, Princess Anne replied, '*Me?*' Ten years further on, the Princess might have remembered her cousin's words when her own engagement to Lieutenant (later Captain) Mark Phillips of the Queen's Dragoon Guards was announced by the Queen and the Duke of Edinburgh.

A champion competitor in all manner of equestrian events, Princess Anne had first met Mark Phillips in 1968, at a reception for the British Olympic Equestrian Team, which she had attended with her grandmother in the City of London. Attracted to the Lieutenant very largely because of his own riding achievements, Princess Anne and he began to meet regularly until the media caught wind of their budding romance and, inevitably, played it up for all it was worth.

A bridesmaid on six occasions – to Lady Pamela Mountbatten, Princess Margaret, the Duchess of Kent, Princess Alexandra, Princess Anne-Marie of Denmark and Lady Elizabeth Anson, respectively – Princess Anne finally became the bride herself, on Wednesday 14 November 1973. It was the event of the year.

In a bleak winter of industrial unrest, the royal wedding provided a brief, but dazzling, respite from the gloom that hung over the country at the time. By dawn on that chilly but bright morning, spectators had been in place along the processional route for hours – some arriving the night before to ensure front-row positions. As the hour of the wedding neared, troops marched from nearby barracks and began to line the Mall, Whitehall, Parliament Street and Broad Sanctuary; bands played martial music mixed with popular tunes to entertain the crowds, and a seemingly endless stream of limousines purred past on their way to the Abbey. Among visiting royalty were Prince Rainier and Princess Grace of Monaco, the ex-King and Queen of Greece, the Crown Prince and Princess of Norway, the Crown Princess (now Queen Beatrix) of the Netherlands and her husband Prince Claus, and the future King and Queen of Spain, Juan Carlos and Sophia, whose own marriage took place less than a year after they had met at the wedding of the Duke and Duchess of Kent at York in 1961.

Within the hour the Abbey had been brought to vibrant life; the royal family seated to one side of the High Altar, the bridegroom and his best man patiently awaiting the arrival of the bride herself. At 11.30 the trumpeters sounded the customary fanfare and, to the hymn, 'Glorious Things of Thee are Spoken', sung by the choir to the tune of the German National Anthem, Princess Anne – dressed in a tudor-inspired gown of ivory silk – proceeded along the nave on the arm of her father.

The emphasis that day very clearly rested on informality, and despite the solemnity that is always present at church weddings great or small, a host of informal touches made the wedding of Princess Anne and Mark Phillips a particularly memorable occasion. As the Queen Mother remarked to the Queen, whilst driving to the Abbey, 'Everybody looks *so* happy.'

Between Princess Anne's wedding in 1973 and the Prince Andrew's in 1986 there were no other royal weddings in the Abbey.

THE
ENGAGEMENT

AFTER SUCH ALARMING NEWS AS LEAKS FROM
NUCLEAR POWER STATIONS, ACTS OF TERRORIST
BRUTALITY, SCENES OF VIOLENCE IN THE CITY
STREETS AND SO ON, IT WAS REFRESHING, INDEED
DELIGHTFUL, TO FIND SO HAPPY A STORY AS THE
ROYAL ENGAGEMENT BRIEFLY DOMINATING THE
HEADLINES. FOR SEVERAL WEEKS NEWSPAPERS HAD
BEEN RUNNING PHOTO-STORIES ABOUT SARAH
FERGUSON, THE LAUGHING, SLIGHTLY DISHEVELLED
'SLOANE' FROM CLAPHAM JUNCTION, AS
SPECULATION ABOUT HER LOVE FOR THE QUEEN'S
SECOND SON GATHERED MOMENTUM.

Until the early 1980s when property prices in London's more fashionable districts started to boom and 'desirable' residences began slipping out of most people's reach, 'undesirable' Battersea, south of the Thames, was something of a no-go area. Then, quite suddenly, a mass exodus began and, in estate agents' jargon, 'Young Professionals', followed by tribes of 'Hooray Henrys' and 'Henriettas', latterly renamed 'Sloane Rangers', packed up their goods and chattels and crossed the river to establish themselves in row upon row of terraced houses, built at the turn of the century with the working man in mind.

Even today, Clapham Junction, which Nell Dunn immortalized twenty years ago in her raunchy novel *Up the Junction* (subsequently filmed, and appropriately premiered, at the Granada, now a bingo hall, on St John's Hill) is a very shabby substitute for Sloane Street. But the area was made more attractive by manageable prices, and before long 'Sloanes' were forsaking the salubrious stuccoed houses of W8, SW3 and SW10, in favour of the narrow, undistinguished streets of Battersea SW11 and Clapham SW4.

In Coronation year, 1953, the Queen took a state drive in an open-topped Daimler through some of these streets, and one evening, a very long time ago, in a small, seedy-looking restaurant on York Road, near Battersea Bridge, Princess Margaret once sang duets with Cleo Laine. Otherwise royal visits, public or private, were never a noticeable feature of life in this part of the metropolis.

However, among those who did come to Clapham Junction was Carolyn Beckwith-Smith, a cousin of both the Princess of Wales's lady-in-waiting, the ubiquitous Anne Beckwith-Smith, and Janey Napier, an extra lady-in-waiting to the Duchess of Kent. She settled in Lavender Gardens, just behind Arding & Hobbs' bargain-basement. Sharing Carolyn's house was Sarah Ferguson, the comely,

Sarah picking up mail at her flat in Clapham Junction

freckle-faced red-head, with whom the Queen's second son fell in love. But for Sarah, Lavender Gardens might never have attracted the attention of the outside world. It would certainly never have been visited by coach-loads of tourists anxious to gaze upon the unprepossessing house where Prince Andrew passed many an idyllic hour.

Until the start of 1986, when the media first caught wind of Prince Andrew's latest romance, Sarah Ferguson was as anonymous as any other resident of that now-famous street. Then, in a replay of the way Lady Diana Spencer was plagued before her, the 'rat-pack' descended *en masse*, armed with cameras, microphones, tape-recorders, video cameras and, of course, a barrage of compromising questions. Unlike Diana Spencer, however, whose Earls Court flat was kept under constant surveillance by the ever-vigilant press corps, Sarah seemed better equipped to look after herself; keeping her nerve, even when chased by a regiment of photographers, packed into a convoy of twenty cars, and maintaining a breezy, if guarded, rapport with those who relentlessly dogged her every step.

Seven weeks later, on Wednesday 19 March, exactly one month after Prince Andrew's twenty-sixth birthday, 'the worst kept secret of the year' was made public. At

Sarah not long before her engagement was announced

10 o'clock that morning, the standard, type-written communiqué, issued by the Buckingham Palace press office, read, 'It is with the greatest pleasure that The Queen and The Duke of Edinburgh announce the betrothal of their beloved son The Prince Andrew to Miss Sarah Ferguson, daughter of Major Ronald Ferguson and Mrs Hector Barrantes.'

At the Palace a group of newsmen waited in the damp, misty garden for the customary photo-call, while inside court correspondents from the BBC and ITV waited among the lights and television cameras to interview the Prince and his fiancée. Outside, beyond the gilt-topped railings, a crowd gathered to soak up the atmosphere. But unlike the day five years before when Prince Charles and Lady Diana became officially engaged,

A witty board outside Sarah's flat after the engagement was announced

Surrounded on all sides by the 'rat pack'

The day before the engagement, Sarah hurrying to work, March 1986

and Earl and Countess Spencer paraded themselves before the crowds at the Palace, Andrew and Sarah's parents chose to keep a very low profile. At his home in Hampshire, Major Ferguson spoke briefly of his delight to waiting reporters, before setting out for Heathrow Airport *en route* for Australia to visit his elder daughter Jane; while Sarah's mother, Susan Barrantes, at home in Argentina, was even less accessible to British news teams.

At noon, meanwhile, Prince Andrew and Miss Ferguson, seated side by side on a brocade sofa, appeared 'live' on television to talk of their romance. In marked contrast to the interview given by the Prince of Wales and his bride-to-be, in February 1981, this interview was not only refreshing for its candour, but for the joking, informal asides, that the couple exchanged.

Sarah's doodles, including a sketch of her ring, during the week of her engagement

Asked when he had asked Sarah to marry him, Prince Andrew replied, '. . . some weeks ago and Sarah actually said "yes", which surprised me. She did say – which is a little anecdote for you – if you wake up tomorrow morning you can tell me it's all a huge joke. I didn't.'

Moments later, when the interviewers asked the couple what they liked about each other, their responses were punctuated with outbursts of laughter:

Sarah: Wit, charm. . . .
HRH: Yes, probably, and the red hair. . . .
Sarah: And the good looks . . . Sorry. . . .

And when asked to describe the ring – a large, oval Burma ruby, surrounded by ten 'drop' diamonds – Sarah smiled and said simply, 'Stunning. I wanted a ruby.'

Half an hour later, arm-in-arm, the Prince and his fiancée walked onto the terrace and down the steps into the Palace garden. There was a public kiss – for the benefit of the media – and then the couple went back inside for more champagne celebrations, this time in private.

Once the engagement was announced, everyone who had been in on the secret breathed more easily. Sarah's step-mother revealed how tense those days before the Palace announcement were for her family. Sarah and Andrew kept their secret for over a month, while the Queen was away, but on Sunday 16 March three days before the news was released, they told their parents and asked their permission.

This was, of course, a courtesy to Sarah's father. In Andrew's case, however, the Prince needed the Queen's formal consent under the terms of the Royal Marriages Act of 1772, and in turn Her Majesty was required to signify her approval at a meeting of the Privy Council.

Understandably both sets of parents were excited and happy to hear the young couple's news. 'Sarah came

Official! Sarah and her Prince on the Terrace at Buckingham Palace

Engagement day at Buckingham Palace

The engagement ring: an oval 'Burma' ruby, surrounded by ten drop diamonds

The bridal pair on the day their engagement was announced

Happy engagement day photographs

An informal study of the Prince and Sarah shortly before their wedding

home on Sunday and in hushed tones told us that Prince Andrew had asked her to marry him,' says Mrs Ferguson.

'I wanted to break open the champagne there and then. Sarah told us we musn't until it was made official on Wednesday. She was terrified even telling us in case something would happen. It was all quite frightening. The next three days were the longest in my life.'

The morning after the announcement, Sarah Ferguson, businesswoman, was back at her office near Hanover Square, in the heart of London's West End. But now, in her capacity as the Queen's prospective daughter-in-law, press harassment had come to an end. As she arrived from Buckingham Palace, she was accompanied by Prince Andrew's personal detective, backed up by two plain clothes officers. All the photographers could do was take their pictures from behind the crash barriers on

Portraits taken to mark the engagement of Andrew and Sarah

the opposite side of the street, under the vigilant eye of a dozen 'bobbies'.

Yet as public excitement began to simmer down, preparations for the royal event of 1986 were already under way behind the stolid, red-brick façade of St James's Palace. State occasions, and that term covers far fewer events than most people imagine, are traditionally managed by the Duke of Norfolk in his role as Hereditary Earl Marshal of England. Royal weddings, however, including that of the Prince and Princess of Wales, with all its pomp and pageantry, are not classed as events of state. This means that the success of *non* state occasions becomes the responsibility of the Lord Chamberlain.

As we saw earlier, that office is currently held by Princess Alexandra's brother-in-law, the tall, silver-haired Earl of Airlie. To him, as 'Impressario of Pageantry to the Queen', Prince Andrew's wedding represented his first major job since succeeding Lord Maclean. His duties, legion and complicated, included the unenviable task of drawing up a provisional guest list which was then submitted to Her Majesty. That list, on which no fewer than 2,000 names appeared, was then returned to the Lord Chamberlain and the invitations, large formal cards, bearing the royal cypher, were duly despatched to friends of the bride and bridegroom, their families (even members of the royal family, according to protocol, are officially invited in the most formal manner), and hosts of people from every walk of life, considered worthy of attending the ceremony.

Once acceptance of those much-coveted invitations was signified, Lord Airlie and his team of fifteen assistants, headed by Sir John Johnston, Comptroller of the Lord Chamberlain's office, tackled the equally unenviable task of drawing up a seating plan, an especially daunting task, given that only 800 guests out of the total congregation of 2,000 were able to see anything of the processions. Fewer still were able to see the ceremony itself, except on the television monitor screens, discreetly erected at intervals along the nave of Westminster Abbey.

On all such occasions, it is certain that the Lord Chamberlain must enjoy the feeling of relief at the knowledge that he is not alone in organizing so monumental an event. To the Home Office and thus to the Commissioner of the Metropolitan Police, for example, falls the task of policing the entire show, even to deploying armed officers, cleverly disguised as footmen, on the back of the royal carriages. The Ministry of Defence must make all arrangements necessary for the participation of the Armed Forces (at Princess Anne's wedding thirteen years ago, 845 soldiers, airmen and sailors were on parade); while the Department of the Environment bears the responsibility for furnishing flag-poles, banners and any other form of 'official' street decorations that might be required.

At Westminster Abbey, the Receiver-General supervises such items as the awning, the hire and delivery of the required 2000 chairs, and the care of the bright blue carpet that extends almost the length of the Abbey itself, from the West Door to the steps of the Sacrarium. Of a more domestic, but certainly no less important nature, arrangements for the wedding reception, or the Wedding Breakfast, as it is properly known, fall to the Master of the Household. As a rule fewer than 200 guests are invited to attend this, the most informal part of any royal wedding. And naturally, once the royal family has returned to Buckingham Palace, informality is indubitably the key-word.

Following the wedding of the Prince and Princess of Wales, for instance, Prince Andrew and Prince Edward – waving noisy football rattles – took it upon themselves to announce some of their parents' guests. 'One King of Norway,' they cried as King Olav appeared, and 'One King of the Hellenes,' as Constantine, the exiled Greek monarch walked in. It will also be remembered that the royal brothers, both of whom acted as Prince Charles's supporters, were responsible for decorating the landau that transported the Prince and Princess of Wales to Waterloo Station at the start of their honeymoon, with heart-shaped, helium-filled balloons, and a huge sheet of card, on which they had daubed the words 'JUST MARRIED'.

Strictly speaking, the term 'Wedding Breakfast' applies only to marriages that are celebrated well before noon. But while royal weddings are invariably late morning affairs, the 'Breakfast' itself doesn't begin until the early afternoon. The result is, of course, luncheon, at which, in order to help facilitate the natural flow of conversation, as well as the buoyant sense of informality, the royal family and their guests sit at individual round tables normally prepared for about twenty people apiece.

Much of the glamour of an event like a royal wedding is, of course, provided by the spectacular pageantry; the troops lining the streets, the glittering escorts furnished by the Household Cavalry (The Life Guards and The Blues and Royals) and the dazzling fleet of royal carriages.

By tradition the royal bride herself rides to her wedding in the Glass Coach. Upholstered in dark blue satin, with the royal coat-of-arms emblazoned on its doors, this picturesque carriage was originally built in 1910 as a sheriff's town coach. A year later it took its place in the Royal Mews in readiness to drive royal guests to the coronation of King George V. As a bridal coach, however, it made its debut at the wedding of Princess Mary in 1922, and in 1923 it transported the present Queen Mother – then the new Duchess of York – from Westminster Abbey to Buckingham Palace. In the years since then, it has been used by most royal brides –

The Glass Coach

The exquisite panelling of the State Coach

The Scottish State Coach and the Glass Coach (centre), flanked by the State Coach and a State Landau

Princess Marina, Princess Alice, Duchess of Gloucester, the present Queen, Princess Margaret, Princess Alexandra, Princess Anne, the Princess of Wales and, of course, the former Miss Sarah Ferguson.

Second only to the State (or Coronation) Coach itself, is the elaborate Irish State Coach. Immediately recognizable as the équipage used by the Queen each time she goes in state to open Parliament, the original coach – which was subsequently destroyed by fire – was bought by Queen Victoria on her second visit to the Dublin Exhibition in 1852. What we see today is an exact replica incorporating the metal portions that survived the blaze.

Yet perhaps the most romantic carriage of the entire royal fleet is the dainty Scottish State Coach. On its doors the Scottish coat-of-arms are represented in gold, crimson, green, white and blue, while on the perspex-panelled roof, a replica of the Scottish State Crown is skirted by an elaborate gilded rail incorporating a thistle motif. Created as recently as 1969, the undercarriage and lower half of the body once formed part of a coach built in 1830 for the Duchess of Teck, mother of Queen Mary. It was subsequently sold to the Earl of Albemarle who, in 1930, gave it to Queen Mary. A completely new top was added seventeen years ago. Housed at the Royal Mews at Windsor Castle, this carriage was last seen in Windsor, when it carried the Queen and 'Prince Philip on a short drive through the town, following the thanksgiving service for Her Majesty's sixtieth birthday, celebrated at St George's Chapel in April 1986.

At the last royal wedding, in a complete break with tradition, the Prince and Princess of Wales returned from St Paul's Cathedral in the scarlet and gold 1902 State Landau. This carriage, seen most frequently at the start of State Visits to London or Windsor, was built for.Prince Andrew's great-great-grand-father King Edward VII and

Queen Alexandra's State Coach. (Below) The royal fleet's pièce de résistance: the State Coach, popularly known as the Coronation Coach

was first used by him on 25 October 1902, when he drove into the City of London.

All these carriages, together with Queen Alexandra's State Coach, the State and semi-State landaus, are kept in the finest condition by staff of the Royal Mews under the direction of the Crown Equerry.

Away from what might be called the ceremonial arrangements for a royal wedding are the private preparations and decisions. Who will the bride be attended by? What flowers will she and her bridesmaids carry? Who will design her going-away outfit? Above all, who will design *the* bridal gown itself and what will it look like, are all questions that must be readily answered. In the past the late Sir Norman Hartnell, who dressed royal ladies for more than forty years, was an obvious candidate. His designs were worn, for example, by Princess Alice, Duchess of Gloucester in 1935, by Princess Elizabeth in 1947, Princess Margaret in 1960 and the present Duchess of Gloucester in 1972. Departures from this almost traditional mould occurred in 1961 when Katharine Worsley (now the Duchess of Kent) commissioned John Cavanagh to design her wedding dress, in 1963 when Princess Alexandra also chose Cavanagh (who had fre-

quently designed outfits for Princess Marina), and in 1973 when Princess Anne asked Maureen Baker of Susan Small, to create her bridal gown.

This year, however, Sarah Ferguson chose someone who was hailed as a complete outsider, although she has in fact made clothes for the Duchess of Kent and the ex-Queen of Greece. Her name was Lindka Cierach. 'Although she may be unknown to most of us,' wrote Jackie Modlinger, Fashion Editor of the *Daily Express*, 'Lindka's name is a byword in the upper-crust society circles in which [Sarah Ferguson] moves.

'From her front-room workshop in Fulham, Lindka has created fairytale frocks for a host of fashionable brides with impressive pedigrees [among them Pandora Stevens, Lady Rose Cecil and Charlotte Monckton]. Each of Lindka's designs is a one-off, and every one different. Her style reflects her customers' wishes, but her dresses often have a sweep of costume drama about them, and feature the delicate beadwork and imaginative necklines which are her hallmark. Lindka's appeal to Fergie must surely be that she believes a woman should dress to suit her own personality, and she is noted for the personal service she provides, rather than adhering to her own dictates or the whims of current fashion. Of one thing we can be sure. The Dress, like its owner, will be an original.'

As well as being original, it was also most probably very expensive. For Lindka's wedding dresses cost at least £5,000 and her evening dresses start at £600.

Yet, if the gown itself was among the most personal decisions which faced Sarah Ferguson, one more consideration ran a near second; the flowers which must always be chosen and designed to complement any bride's overall appearance. In this case, Sarah chose another outsider. Jane Packer, a florist who runs her own shop off Oxford Street, created the pretty knot of blue muscari and lilies of the valley which Sarah wore when she joined members

Lindka Cierach at work in Fulham

Sarah helping to collect daffodils for the Queen, 21 April 1986

of the royal family at the Royal Opera House on 21 April, for the gala evening held to celebrate the Queen's birthday. Delighted with the result, she immediately asked Jane to prepare her bridal bouquet. 'When I heard about the wedding,' she said, 'I thought naturally that it would be nice to do the flowers – but I never dreamed for a moment I would be picked.' She was and, as we now know, Sarah's choice could scarcely have been bettered.

For Sarah Ferguson, who was hounded by the press for weeks before her engagement was announced, becoming acclimatized to public appearances must, at least in some respects, have seemed a more sedate affair. At Windsor, her first formal appearance was with the royal family when they attended matins at St George's Chapel on Easter Sunday. Three weeks later, dressed in a grey suit designed with an unusual bustle effect, she and Prince Andrew drove through the rain to attend the Queen's birthday service. That afternoon, as 6,000 school children serenaded the Queen with a specially composed song, 'Happy Birthday Ma'am', Sarah joined Her Majesty,

Prince Philip and Prince Andrew on the Buckingham Palace balcony and later helped to collect the thousands of daffodils from the young singers massed below in the forecourt. To round off that memorable day, Sarah – dressed in cream, blue and black satin – joined her future in-laws at Covent Garden and won a special ovation from the crowds waiting outside to cheer the royal party. More informally, Andrew and Sarah shared the royal box with the Queen at the Windsor Horse Show in early May, and just a week or two later, as if enough was enough for the time being, Sarah left England's cold, wet spring behind her to fly out to Antigua for a week's holiday in the welcome Caribbean sunshine.

She flew to the West Indies with her detective to stay with an old school-friend Florence Belmondo, daughter of French film star Jean-Paul Belmondo. There she swam, sunbathed and dieted – as she was anxious to lose some weight – eating the light, delicious food that is so easily found in the Caribbean: fruit and fish.

Although even on that faraway island of Antigua Sarah was followed by news reporters and photographers,

Sarah, deep in thought

again she showed an easy talent for coping with such pressures. When reporters turned up at the Admiral Inn restaurant where she was enjoying dinner of grilled king fish with her girl-friend, she sent a waiter with two pink lilies over to their table. 'Please accept these flowers from the lady with her love,' was the message.

Sarah called out: 'Sorry I can't run to champagne!'

The reporters, in their turn, sent over a bottle of champagne which Sarah drank happily, raising her glass to them: 'Enjoy yourselves,' she laughed.

As she was leaving, Sarah brought the half-empty bottle back. 'I'm sorry,' she said, 'we can't finish it.' In reply to Press representatives who apologized for disturbing her evening, she said: 'There was no problem. We anticipated we would run into each other some time. We had a very enjoyable meal and I appreciated the way you handled it.' She flew home next day for a joyous reunion with Andrew.

Tanned and happy, Sarah inspected the latest batch of presents which had arrived at Buckingham Palace from all parts of the world. Most had already been unpacked by the Queen's on-duty lady-in-waiting and all had a thorough inspection by security experts, including 'sniffer' dogs, before arriving in the royal apartments. In their typically unselfish way Sarah and Andrew had already decided to ask people (other than personal friends and family) wishing to send gifts to send a donation instead to the King George's Jubilee Trust.

'A very sweet and generous gesture. It has never happened before,' said an official of the Trust which helps children suffering from fatal and crippling diseases. Proceeds from the official souvenir programme will also go to the Trust, but presents from old friends like Nancy Reagan will, of course, be gladly accepted. Mrs Reagan, wife of the American President, met Sarah when Andrew escorted her to polo at the time of the Prince and Princess of Wales's wedding.

Then, on Saturday 7 June, shortly after her return, Sarah and Prince Andrew attended their first official engagement together, when they visited Weymouth to attend a Royal Gala night held in aid of the King George's Fund for Sailors at the Pavilion Theatre.

Prince Andrew undertook one public engagement during the weeks preceding the wedding which under-

In the Caribbean, away from it all

The couple's first official engagement: visiting Weymouth

Sporting a black and white bow in her hair: Sarah, summer 1986

Sarah at the 1986 Chelsea Flower Show

lined the serious, thoughtful side of his character. Speaking at a fund-raising lunch on the fortieth anniversary of the Outward Bound Trust, a favourite charity of Prince Philip and his sons, which organizes adventure training for youngsters, he attacked the misuse of drugs, alchohol, violent TV and films.

In a speech carefully thought out and written by himself Prince Andrew recalled how he was only just appreciating the benefits of the Outward Bound training he had received at Gordonstoun which, at the time, had 'seemed dotty to the sixteen- and seventeen-year-olds'.

The Trust, he said, offered a 'countervailing force

The Prince and his fiancée only weeks before their wedding. (Right) Andrew and Sarah at Smith's Lawn, June 1986

for good against the pollution of the moral environment which so endangers young people today.

'Moral pollution may well be a strong phrase to use but I feel that it is justified, particularly when you look at the amount of gratuitous violence purveyed on television and in the cinema in the name of entertainment; when, too, you contemplate the increasing availability of drugs and misuse of alcohol and when the two influences combine to cause acts of criminal ferocity.'

It was strong, hard-hitting stuff which provoked some criticism. But it was a speech indicating the Prince was not prepared to tread an easy-going royal path.

On the same day, in an interview that appeared in the magazine *Woman's Own*, the Duke of Edinburgh denied reports that he was 'extremely grateful' his son was to marry Sarah Ferguson. 'That sounds as if I were afraid he had not been going in the right direction which is absolutely not true.

'I'm delighted he's getting married, but not because I think it will keep him out of trouble because, in fact, he's never been in trouble in the sense the popular press would have it,' he said.

'They seem very happy,' added Prince Philip. 'I think that Sarah will be a great asset.'

Sarah with Princess Margaret at Ascot, June 1986

An elegant Sarah with her fiancé at Ascot in June 1986

At Ascot, June 1986

WEDNESDAY 23 JULY

FOR SOME 500 MILLION PEOPLE DISPERSED
THROUGHOUT THE WORLD, THE WEDDING OF THEIR
ROYAL HIGHNESSES THE DUKE AND DUCHESS OF YORK
WAS A SPECTACULAR OCCASION, ENCOMPASSING ALL
THAT IS BEST IN BRITISH ROYAL TRADITION. FOR THE
BRIDE AND BRIDEGROOM, THE POMP TOOK SECOND
PLACE TO THE INTENSELY PERSONAL COMMITMENT
THEY MADE ONE TO THE OTHER BEFORE THE
HIGH ALTAR OF WESTMINSTER ABBEY.

The Queen and Prince Philip leave Buckingham Palace

At 8 a.m. on royal wedding day, some three hours before the trumpet fanfares stilled the voices of the congregation in Westminster Abbey, came the news eagerly anticipated by royal historians: the bridegroom was no longer merely a prince, but a royal duke – His Royal Highness The Duke of York. Thus his bride, who entered the Abbey as the relatively lowly Miss Sarah Ferguson, emerged one hour later, not as Princess Andrew, as most would have expected, but as Her Royal Highness The Duchess of York.

What, one wonders, were the thoughts of the Duke's grandmother, Queen Elizabeth The Queen Mother, as she watched from her gilt chair in the Sacrarium? This wedding, more than any other, aroused emotions un-dimmed by the passage of time. For on 26 April 1923, the then Lady Elizabeth Bowes Lyon had stood in exactly the same place as Sarah Ferguson at the High Altar during her own wedding to Prince Albert, Duke of York, the second son of King George V and Queen Mary. Sixty-three years later the wedding of Andrew and Sarah, Duke and Duchess of York, evoked the spirit of that earlier York wedding.

Despite the searching eyes of a battery of media cameras, to say nothing of a remote-controlled camera at the High Altar, and a worldwide television audience estimated at between three and five million, it was apparent that, to the bride and bridegroom, the rest of the world had been forgotten. By the very nature of their personalities the new Duke and Duchess were relaxed and self-confident enough to turn this enormously public occasion into something that was essentially private and, above all, their own. Indeed, all who witnessed the royal wedding shared a common sense of happiness that was far removed from the problems of the world. To quote the *Daily Mail*, the day belonged 'to all of us, for all are invited to share their joy; to switch off for a few blissful happy hours all that ceaseless chatter of "crises" and of "rifts". The complete reverse? The day [was] reserved for the celebration of love and marriage. And if that is not the very heart of things, then we don't know what it is that makes the world go round.'

Beneath skies that were alternately overcast then brilliantly sunny, London assumed a carnival-like mood on the wedding day itself. Despite the fact that 23 July was not a public holiday, the processional route was densely packed by cheering, celebrating crowds. The infectious spirit was matched by the delighted smiles of the royal family and, particularly, the Queen and Prince Philip. A scarlet ribbon of guardsmen in impeccable order lined the route back to back with over 3,000 policemen drawn from all over Britain who faced inwards to the crowds – symbols of the vast security mantle that enveloped the wedding route. The gold, silver and scarlet of the mounted escort of the Household Cavalry trans-fused an eddy of vivid colour into the streets of the capital, lined by Union Jacks and bunting. At 10.57 precisely, the Queen, dressed by Ian Thomas in stunning delphinium blue silk crêpe with a matching hat stitched with organza peonies, rode with her family in a procession of semi-State Landaus to Westminster Abbey.

There, for more than an hour, the congregation of almost 2,000 guests had been assembling in a great flowering of personalities from all over the world. Nancy Reagan, for example, dressed in pistachio green, represented her husband and the American nation, while among the more recognizable foreign royal guests were Felipe, Prince of the Asturias, and his sisters Elena and

The Queen Mother, the last Duchess of York, with Princess Margaret

The Queen and the Duke of Edinburgh in the semi-State Landau wave to the crowds

Christina, who represented their parents the King and Queen of Spain; present too was the exiled Greek King Constantine and his family. Gradually the Abbey – festooned as never before with some 20,000 lilies, roses, carnations, gladioli and Tokyo chrysanthemums, in a riot of colours from pink, white and cream to palest yellow – filled with guests, both distinguished and humble, brought together by the lives of Sarah and Andrew. Among the more recognizable non-royal guests were celebrities such as pop singer Elton John, racing driver Jackie Stewart and comedians Billy Connolly and Pamela Stephenson. Outside, beyond the blue and white awning decorated with the bridal couple's entwined initials worked in cream flowers, an immeasurable congregation of spectators, closely monitored by the Metropolitan Police on close-circuit television, joined the wider viewing audience, as witnesses to this particularly appealing royal wedding.

At 11.05, eight minutes after the departure of his mother's carriage from Buckingham Palace, Lieutenant His Royal Highness The Duke of York, RN, dressed in naval uniform, accompanied by his younger brother Prince Edward, acting as his 'supporter', as the Best Man is known in royal circles, left the Palace riding in the 1902 State Landau, decorated with nosegays of white roses of York and sporting a lucky silver horseshoe.

Without a trace of nerves, the young Duke and his brother, dressed in the uniform of a Royal Marine Lieutenant, waved and grinned broadly in response to the crowd's enthusiastic welcome. As he arrived at the West Door of the Abbey, the crowd burst spontaneously into a rousing chorus of the old nursery rhyme, 'The Grand Old Duke of York'. Doubtless the children's song was familiar to the eight 'Little People', as Sarah called her attendants. For a moment, as the royal family arrived and processed along the Nave, the four brides-maids, together with the quartet of pages, waited with

The two brothers. Andrew in naval uniform and Edward, an acting lieutenant in th

...oyal Marines

Sarah and her father leaving Clarence House

the Ferguson family Nanny, Linda Tucker, in a side chapel. The small girls, Zara Phillips, daughter of Princess Anne; Alice Ferguson, the bride's half-sister; Laura Fellowes, niece of the Princess of Wales, and Lady Rosanagh Innes-Ker, daughter of the Duke and Duchess of Roxburghe, wore enchanting ballerina-length dresses of palest peach taffeta over petticoats of ivory Nottingham lace, and carried hoops of flowers instead of the more customary posies. Complementing them were the page boys, Prince William of Wales and Seamus Makim, nephews of the bride and bridegroom, dressed in sailor suits modelled on that worn in 1846 by the future Edward VII on the then Victorian royal yacht. The two elder boys, Peter Phillips and Andrew Ferguson wore midshipman's dress, based on uniforms of 1782.

The scene was now set for the eagerly awaited arrival of the bride herself. Waiving every young woman's right to keep her bridegroom waiting for a few minutes, the Glass Coach set out from Clarence House precisely according to schedule. The time was 11.15. For those gathered opposite the tall black gates of the Queen Mother's official residence, where the bride – like Lady Diana Spencer before her – had spent the previous night, this was the moment they had looked forward to, not least for a first glimpse of the bridal gown. As Sarah had put it on on the eve of the wedding, there would 'never be a dress to match it'. She was absolutely right. Designer Lindka Cierach has always maintained that she insists on bringing to her gowns some of the personality of the bride who wears them. From heavy ivory duchess satin, almost champagne in its glowing tone, Lindka had created for Sarah a renaissance silhouette, tapering from full-crowned shoulders to a pearl-edged point at the elbow and waist. The underskirt bordered by a silk scalloped lace flounce billowed out the heavy sheen of the satin skirt. The designer's hallmark – heavy beading – was never seen to more dramatic

Lady Rosanagh Innes-Ker and Zara Phillips arrive at the Abbey

from a cutting which had formed part of Queen Victoria's bridal bouquet in 1840.

Accompanied by her father Major Ronald Ferguson, in whose honour, as a former commander of the Sovereign's Escort of the Household Cavalry, the Queen approved an escort of six troopers of the Life Guards, the bride drove to the Abbey in the romantic Glass Coach. Only the night before Sarah had said in a television interview that she fully intended to enjoy her

Lindka Cierach's design for the back of the bridal gown

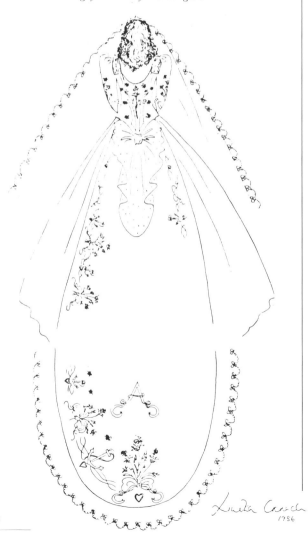

effect than on Sarah's wedding dress. On the train, 17 feet 6 in. in length, which cascaded from a large fan-shaped bow, were the thistles and bees of the bride's coat-of-arms, together with anchors, waves and hearts, complemented by her bridegroom's initial, all magnificently worked in seed pearls and *diamanté*. Securing her scalloped edged veil of silk tulle, embroidered with true lovers' knots and shimmering with sequins, was a headdress of fresh flowers – roses, lily petals, gardenias and lilies-of-the-valley. However, secretly Sarah had organized a surprise: at the end of the ceremony, to symbolize her metamorphosis from commoner into Duchess of York (and therefore the senior royal Duchess), the flowers were carefully removed to reveal a diamond tiara which, loaned by an unidentified friend, represented the traditional 'something borrowed'. Further enhancing the unsurpassed floral theme of this wedding, the royal bride carried a fragrant 'S'-shaped spray of cream lilies, palest yellow roses, gardenias, lilies-of-the-valley and the now traditional sprig of myrtle, from a bush grown

Dress designer Lindka Cierach arranges the bride's train before the service

wedding day; and there could be no doubt at all that she was fulfilling that promise as she sat in her carriage, turning from left to right, acknowledging the crowds' cheers with an inexperienced, almost self-conscious wave. On the arm of her father, who had pronounced himself to be a 'fantastically proud' man, Sarah entered the Abbey and stood for a moment inside the garlanded West Door as her train was carefully arranged and the twenty-two Royal Marine trumpeters sounded a fanfare. Like nearly every father of nearly every bride, 'Major Ronald' smiled and joked with his daughter as they began their four-minute walk up the Nave and under the ornate organ screen bedecked with creamy-white madonna lilies, to the steps of the persian-carpeted Sacrarium, where, on the north and south sides of the altar, the families of the bride and bridegroom proudly

A magnificent view of the train as Sarah and her father enter the Nave

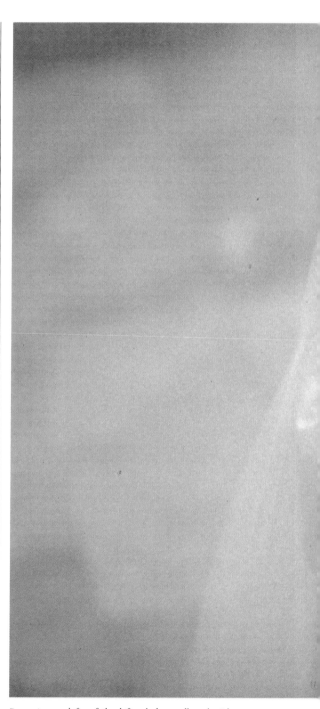

Reassuring words from father before the long walk up the aisle

faced each other. Composed and smiling, Sarah won a grin of delight from her bridegroom as she approached, and side by side they moved towards the rose-damask prayer-desks where they exchanged their vows.

As the Dean of Westminster, Dr Michael Mayne, who assumed office only two weeks earlier, stepped forward to open the marriage service, it seemed for a moment as if the television arc-lamps and the Abbey's famous Waterford crystal chandeliers fused together to irradiate the very considerable splendour of the scene, accentuating the rich tones of the wine red and gold velvet backdrop to the High Altar itself, the copes and mantles of the clergy, and the jewelled orders and uniforms of the military personnel. Having given her

bouquet – the gift of the Worshipful Company of Gardeners – to the temporary care of Lady Rosanagh Innes-Ker, her senior bridesmaid, the vivacious young woman who was about to become Duchess of York folded her hands in front of her as the Archbishop of Canterbury, Dr Robert Runcie, began, 'I require and charge you both, as ye will answer at the dreadful day of judgement when the secrets of all hearts shall be disclosed, that if either of you know any impediment, why ye may not be lawfully joined together in matrimony, ye do now confess it. For be ye well assured, that so many as are coupled together otherwise than God's word doth allow are not joined together by God; neither is their matrimony lawful.'

The Queen looks on as the Archbishop of Canterbury conducts the service

The bride and groom with Major Ferguson during the ceremony

As the Archbishop's awe-inspiring charge was heard by the congregation – which included many celebrated divorcees – there was a moment's pause before Dr Runcie continued: 'Andrew Albert Christian Edward, wilt thou have this woman to thy wedded wife. . . .' In the same firm tone of voice with which he took his vows only seconds later, Andrew, Duke of York, replied, 'I will.' Then turning to the bride, the Archbishop asked, 'Sarah Margaret, wilt though have this Man to thy wedded husband. . . . Wilt thou obey him, and serve him, love, honour and keep him, in sickness and in health; and, forsaking all other, keep thee only unto him, so long as ye both shall live?'

As firmly as her bridegroom had replied, Sarah responded, 'I will', in a determined voice. That the new Duchess had chosen to 'obey' her husband, whereas the Princess of Wales had elected to 'cherish' her prince, rested on a 'moral' decision, rather than on 'physical' considerations. Sarah had explained that in any kind of conflict, for instance, she would look to her husband for the final, decisive word. Thus, when seen in that light, she would be an 'obedient' wife. She added, however,

Prince William and his cousin Laura Fellowes grow restless during the service

that in all other respects, she had a will of her own, and she and her husband would continue to work in unison or as the 'good team' she pronounced them to be at the time of their engagement.

Only once did Sarah stumble over her words – a second's hesitation when pronouncing the Duke's third name, Christian. From then on all was plain sailing. The bridal couple exchanged rings; Dr Runcie blessed them as man and wife; the Prince of Wales read the Lesson from *Ephesians*; and the choir led the congregation in the hymn 'Lead us, Heavenly Father, lead us'.

Like the wedding of the Prince and Princess of Wales at St Paul's Cathedral five years earlier, an inter-denominational tone was added to the wedding of the new Duke and Duchess of York by the prayers that were offered by the Roman Catholic Archbishop of Westminster; the Moderator of the General Assembly of the Church of Scotland, and the Moderator of the Free Church Federal Council. Finally, when the sound of the National Anthem had subsided, bride and bridegroom made their way into the Chapel of St Edward the Confessor. There, as Felicity Lott sang Mozart's

Laudate Dominum, followed by Arleen Auger's rendition of *Exultate jubilate*, the royal couple signed the marriage registers, the flowers and veil that had covered the bride's face were removed and, as the strains of yet another fanfare filled the Abbey, Their Royal Highnesses The Duke and Duchess of York stepped back into the Sacrarium – the Duke bowing, and his bride curtseying to the Queen.

Informality and royal splendour were equal partners on this day of days and, as the bridal couple made their way back along the Nave, this was particularly evident in the way the Duchess of York greeted those she recognized, with a familiar wide-eyed look and broad grin. Then from Westminster Abbey, the newly weds travelled back to Buckingham Palace in the 1902 State Landau, and *en route* found themselves showered with rice and confetti by delighted spectators.

Not long afterwards as the crowds filled the Mall, eagerly approaching the palace railings for the traditional balcony appearance, Albert Watson, more famous for

The new Duchess of York curtsies to the Queen. (Right) *The Duke and Duchess of York pass beneath the floral arch of the organ screen*

The bride and bridegroom acknowledging the cheers of the crowds in Parliament Square

Followed by a Captain's Escort of the Household Cavalry, the bridal carriage in the Mall

The Queen and Major Ferguson returning along the Mall

On the return journey Prince Philip was accompanied by Susan Barrantes

The Prince and Princess of Wales return to Buckingham Palace

his work in *Vogue*, among other magazines, than for royal portraiture, was busily recording Andrew and Sarah's special day with a series of official wedding photographs, taken in the Throne Room. Then, of course, before the wedding breakfast of diced lobster, prawns, and Scotch lamb; Piesporter 1976, Böllinger Champagne and Graham's Port, came the balcony appearance. 'Kiss her, kiss her!' the crowds yelled. 'Can't hear!' the bride jokingly called back in the style that has very genuinely endeared her to the nation; but the request needed no repeating and, to cheers and whistles, the bride and bridegroom happily embraced. After a few minutes, during which the Duke and Duchess were joined by the entire royal family – the ladies wittingly or unwittingly dressed predominantly in various shades of blue – the balcony appearances were over, the tall glass doors were closed, and the net curtains finally drawn.

By teatime, the crowds had re-assembled to cheer the bridal couple on the first leg of their honeymoon

Oblivious to all the excitement, a small boy sleeps

The royal family and their guests join the bride and bridegroom in the Throne Room at Buckingham Palace. (Front row) seated left to right; the Earl of Ulster, Lady Davina and Lady Rose Windsor, Andrew Ferguson, Lady Rosanagh Innes-Ker, Zara Phillips, Prince William of Wales, Laura Fellowes, Seamus Makim, Alice Ferguson, Peter Phillips, Lady Gabriella Windsor, Lord Frederick Windsor. (Second row) Lady Sarah Armstrong-Jones, Princess Margaret, Princess Anne, the Princess of Wales, holding Prince Harry, the Queen Mother, The Queen, the Duke and Duchess of York, Major Ronald Ferguson, Prince Edward, Mrs Susan Barrantes, the Honourable Mrs Doreen Wright, Mrs Jane Makim. Slightly behind them – Lady Elmhirst, Major Bryan Wright, Alexander Makim. (Third row) Viscount Linley, Captain Mark Phillips, Miss Marina Ogilvy, the Prince of Wales, Princess Alexandra, the Duke of Edinburgh, Princess Michael of Kent, Princess Alice, Duchess of Gloucester, the Duchess of Gloucester, the Duchess of Kent, Lady Helen Windsor. (Back row) James Ogilvy, Prince Michael of Kent, the Honourable Angus Ogilvy, the Duke of Gloucester, the Duke of Kent, and the Earl of St Andrews

'What's that? Can't hear you!' mouths Sarah to the crowds

At last — they kiss, to the delight of the crowds

The Duke of York helps with his bride's train as they leave the balcony

journey to the Azores. Shortly after 4 p.m. amid a storm of rose petals – no less than 24,000 had been specially gathered – the 13th Duke of York and his bride emerged from the Palace in a semi-State Landau, decorated with masts, flags, a model satellite dish and a slogan which read, 'PHONE HOME'. Hitching a free ride was a vast toy teddy bear, a blue ribbon tied around his neck. Now casually dressed in a blue and white silk dress, her titian hair (as the bridegroom described it) blowing in the breeze, the Duchess of York enthusiastically joined her husband in waving to the royal family who chased the carriage out into the palace forecourt.

Travelling through Victoria and Pimlico, the Duke and Duchess arrived at the Royal Hospital in Chelsea, from where they were flown in a helicopter of the Queen's flight to Heathrow Airport. There they climbed aboard the Queen's newest jet aircraft for their honeymoon flight out to meet the Royal Yacht *Britannia* and a cruise that was still a closely guarded secret, even as the jet's back flaps opened to reveal the traditional message 'JUST MARRIED', painted within.

The wedding of the year had passed without a hitch and had delighted a worldwide audience of millions. But let us now close this souvenir book by recalling something the Archbishop of Canterbury said about the Duke and Duchess of York: 'They both have a fine sense of humour. They are blessed with an unusual mixture of exhilaration and steadiness. It should stand them in good stead in their marriage as well as in their public life together.'

The Queen, Princess Margaret and other wedding guests wave farewell to the newly weds

Sarah throws an armful of confetti to the crowd

Prince Edward's contribution to the honeymoon carriage – 'Phone Home' from the film ET